DATE DUE

DEVIANCY

The Psychology
of Being Different

SOCIAL PSYCHOLOGY

A series of monographs, treatises, and texts

Edited by

Leon Festinger and Stanley Schachter

Jack W. Brehm, A Theory of Psychological Reactance. 1966

Ralph L. Rosnow and Edward J. Robinson (Eds.), Experiments in Persuasion. 1967

Jonathan L. Freedman and Anthony N. Doob, Deviancy: The Psychology of Being Different. 1968

Paul G. Swingle, Experiments in Social Psychology. 1968

In preparation

E. Earl Baughman and W. Grant Dahlstrom; Negro and White Children: A Psychological Study in the Rural South

Anthony G. Greenwald, Timothy C. Brock, and Thomas M. Ostrom, Psychological Foundations of Attitudes

DEVIANCY
The Psychology of Being Different

JONATHAN L. FREEDMAN
and ANTHONY N. DOOB

DEPARTMENT OF PSYCHOLOGY
STANFORD UNIVERSITY
STANFORD, CALIFORNIA

ACADEMIC PRESS NEW YORK AND LONDON 1968

ACADEMIC PRESS INC.
111 Fifth Avenue, New York, New York 10003

United Kingdom Edition published by
ACADEMIC PRESS INC. (LONDON) LTD.
Berkeley Square House, London W.1

LIBRARY OF CONGRESS CATALOG CARD NUMBER: 68-14666

PRINTED IN THE UNITED STATES OF AMERICA

PREFACE

This book describes a series of studies concerning the effect of deviancy on behavior. Society is composed of a multitude of deviants. Negroes, geniuses, mental defectives, poets, hippies, the far left and right constitute deviant groups that are integral parts of our society. In addition, almost everyone occasionally finds himself deviant from the groups he is in and we are thus all at times deviants. How deviancy affects a person's behavior and the behavior of others toward him are accordingly ubiquitous and always timely questions. At the moment there are few answers.

The importance of the problem has by no means gone unappreciated. There is an extensive literature on deviancy which includes many different kinds of work ranging from novelistic descriptions to experimental studies. Although we have been greatly helped by this work, our research differs from it in several important respects. In the first place, this earlier work tends to deal with particular types of deviancy. Articles concern the life of the Negro in America, the personality of the criminal, or the development of a genius. They concentrate on one specific kind of deviant rather than dealing with questions involving deviancy in general. Second, almost all of this work is based on observations of actual deviants. Members of the particular deviant group are observed either in the field or in a more controlled situation, but they are already deviants.

Our research is somewhat different. We have tried to study the effect of deviancy per se, without regard to the particular deviant characteristic. In order to do this, we have produced feelings of deviancy by an experimental manipulation and we have avoided specifying the exact nature of the deviancy. Individuals are made to feel deviant and their behavior is compared to others who do not feel deviant. In this way we hoped to investigate the effect of deviancy on behavior in a relatively well-controlled environment from which contaminating factors such as the nature of the particular deviant characteristic and the personality of the deviant were removed.

The research was begun without any clear theoretical underpinnings. We had some vague notions about what the major concerns of a deviant might be, and some ideas about what kinds of behavior deviancy should affect. But we did not have a firm theoretical position to test—the work was admittedly empirical in nature. We wanted to discover how deviancy affected behavior and we simply set out to do this in a wide variety of areas.

We would like to thank Merrill Carlsmith and Dennis and Judy Regan for the helpful ideas, criticisms, and suggestions which they proposed in our many discussions; Leon Festinger who read the whole manuscript and made thoughtful and original comments which enabled us to improve it greatly; and Mary Hoadley, Townsend Brady, and Larry Lanpher for serving as able and ingenious confederates in several experiments. We are also grateful to the National Science Foundation which gave partial support to some of the studies described here, and to the National Institute of Health which provided a fellowship for Anthony N. Doob during two years of this work.

JONATHAN L. FREEDMAN

December, 1967   ANTHONY N. DOOB

CONTENTS

vii

CONTENTS

DEVIANCY

The Psychology
of Being Different

1
THE PROBLEM

Deviancy is a universal attribute. If we define it simply as being very different from the surrounding cultural and statistical norms, almost everybody is and feels deviant at one time or another. There are those who must almost always feel this way. In our society the midget, giant, idiot, genius, Negro, and albino will feel deviant much of the time because they are in fact different from most other people. But those who do not have such unusual characteristics will also sometimes find themselves in a group or situation in which they are different. The White Anglo-Saxon Protestant, who is often considered and may think of himself as the typical American, may find himself walking in an all Negro, Jewish, or Polish neighborhood. Or he may take a trip to Japan and find that everyone speaks another language and that he is stared at by passersby because of his white skin and Western features. The person of average intelligence serving as a reporter at a conference of Nobel prize winners, the person with normal vision at a home for the blind, the man of average height on a professional basketball court must all feel deviant. Whenever someone is different from the rest of the group he is in, he is at least for the moment a deviant.

It is important to note that the absolute value or nature of the deviant characteristic is irrelevant as far as the extent of the deviancy is concerned. Virtually any characteristic can be deviant if it is not shared by the rest of the comparison group. It does not matter if the characteristic is generally considered positive or negative. Gulliver was as deviant among the Brobdingnags when he was unimaginably small and weak as when he lived in Lilliput where he was fantastically big and powerful. The genius is as deviant as the idiot; the girl with a huge bust as the girl with no bust at all; the strong man who can bend steel bars as the weakling who can hardly hold a pencil. It is perhaps remarkable that the term "exceptional" children is used to refer not only to the unusually intelligent, but also to the mentally retarded, the physically handicapped, the emotionally disturbed and so on. Regardless of the content or valence of the critical attribute, deviancy consists simply of being different from the surrounding norms.

We are not suggesting that deviancy be defined in purely statistical terms. The individual's feeling of deviancy and other people's perception of deviancy will depend on the particular dimension, the situation, and the people that are involved. On some dimensions a person may be very different from the norm without being considered or considering himself deviant; whereas on other dimensions, even slight differences may be enough to produce deviancy. Although we have no data on this, we think that for most people quite sizable deviations from the norm in height, intelligence, income, or ability would be necessary to produce deviancy; whereas any physical deformity, criminal record, or sexual deviation would be sufficient to make someone a deviant. Certainly this will vary considerably as a function of the people making the judgments and the situations in which they are being made. The important point is that if someone is different enough on any dimension regardless of whether the difference is evaluated positively or negatively he will be considered and consider himself a deviant.

It was our assumption at the beginning of this work that such feelings of deviancy would have important effects on people's behavior. By this we meant that regardless of the particular way in which someone was deviant, the dimension on which he was different, or whether he was at the positive or negative end of that dimension, the feeling of deviancy per se will produce certain behavior. The particular way in which someone is deviant will, of course, have enormous influence on him; but superimposed on these effects, cutting across all types of deviants, will be deviancy itself. Everyone who feels deviant will to some extent be affected in the same way and have certain behavior in common.

In other words, we are arguing that deviancy is an important dimension which is in some sense unitary. Just as people vary on height, intelligence, need achievement and many other dimensions, they also vary on deviancy. And just as these other factors are thought to have profound and consistent effects on behavior, so deviancy will.

This book describes a series of studies which attempt to discover how the feeling of deviancy influences behavior, and how people who do not share this feeling differ from those who do. It further investigates how people differ in their treatment of deviants and nondeviants. We have not studied types of deviants or specific deviant groups, but rather have tried to study deviancy per se. We have attempted to manipulate deviancy experimentally — making some people feel deviant and others nondeviant; we have tried to do this without telling the people in what way they are deviant nor whether they are at the positive or negative end of the relevant dimension. In this way we hoped to discover the effects of simply thinking you are deviant without regard to the specific effects of any given deviant characteristic.

The experimental program described in this book is primarily empirical in nature. The basic orientation was nontheoretical.

We were concerned chiefly with investigating and specifying some of the effects of deviancy on behavior. Although this approach seems to be somewhat suspect these days, we felt that it was appropriate in this context. Virtually nothing is known about the problem to be studied here, and we, at least, had no theoretical position to defend. The plan of research, therefore, was to select a number of important phenomena which seemed likely to be affected by feelings of deviancy, and simply to see what happened.

Having said this, however, let us note that we did not begin the work in a vacuum—far from it. There has been a great deal of writing, speculating, and even some research on deviancy. Although, as we shall see, most of this work was not directly relevant to our problem, it did provide a number of important hints and suggestions which served as a starting point for our experimentation. It would be neither useful nor practical to present an exhaustive review of all remotely relevant research. Let us instead describe the kinds of work that have been done and attempt to give the flavor of these previous approaches to the problem of deviancy in general.

There are several quite different types of literature which are relevant to a study of deviancy. By far the largest segment is made up of books or articles that are devoted entirely to one particular deviant group. "Prostitution" by Kingsley Davis (1961), *The Negro in the United States* by Franklin E. Frazier (1957), *Genetic Studies of Genius* by Lewis M. Terman and his associates (1925), and *The Eternal Stranger: A Study of Jewish Life in the Small Community* by Benjamin Kaplan (1957) are a few of the thousands of such works. Negroes, Jews, Catholics, homosexuals, criminals, prostitutes, geniuses, the blind, and practically any other deviant groups one could imagine have been described in at least one book of this sort.

The kinds of data on which these books are based vary enormously. At one extreme are novels or narratives based on the author's own experiences, anecdotes, or other relatively personal, nonrigorous evidence. At the other extreme are books or articles based in large part on survey and census data or relatively controlled observations. Although it is generally possible to have somewhat more confidence in the generality and reliability of the more rigorous work, it seems as usual that the other work is considerably richer in detail.

All of these books tend to have in common an emphasis on describing the personality, behavior, and daily lives of the members of the deviant group. What kinds of people are they? What special problems do they face (e.g., getting jobs, discrimination)? How are they different from or similar to people who do not have their deviant characteristics? There is also some attention paid to the question, where appropriate, of how and why they became members of the group. This is particularly pronounced in work on homosexuality, criminality, drug addiction, and other types of deviancy which are strongly rejected by the rest of society.

In addition to this material on particular kinds of deviants, there is a sizable literature written chiefly by sociologists on the topic of "deviance" in general. The conception of deviancy found in this work differs somewhat from ours in that it tends to have a clearly negative connotation and to include primarily people who are not accepted by society, who deviate from society by virtue of antisocial behavior, or who are unable to adjust to society. For example, in a textbook on the sociology of deviant behavior, Clinard states:

> Deviations from norms which are tolerated or which provoke only mild disapproval are obviously of little concern to a society. Only those situations in which behavior is in a disapproved direction, and of sufficient degree to

exceed the tolerance limit of the community, constitute deviant behavior
as it will be used here [Clinard, 1963; p. 22].

Similarly, Becker (1963) writes, "The statistical definition of
deviancy, in short, is too removed from the concern with rule-
breaking which prompts scientific study of outsiders [p. 5]."
In line with this kind of definition of the field, sociologists tend
to limit the category of deviants to criminals, the mentally ill,
addicts, alcoholics, and homosexuals. Occasionally other groups
such as jazz musicians (Becker, 1963) are for some reason included, but even ethnic minorities such as Negroes are generally
treated separately.

Sociologists also tend to concentrate on the question of why
people become or act deviant. Since their major concern is
with the disruption of society supposedly caused by deviant
behavior, it is not surprising that most of their attention is paid
to the etiology and prevention of such behavior. This work thus
tells us relatively little about the deviants themselves or about
how others treat them.

Although this approach is quite different from ours, and the
definition of deviancy much more limited, the fact that such
diverse groups as criminals, the mentally ill, and homosexuals
are discussed in the same terms indicates that sociologists share
our belief that different types of deviants have much in common.
We have been unable to find an explicit statement to this effect,
but this assumption appears to be implicit in much of this work.

Closely related to, but somewhat distinct from this approach,
is the work on so-called "marginality" (e.g., Stonequist, 1937).
Anthropologists and sociologists have been concerned with the
problems faced by people who have not found or cannot accept
a clear role in society. Generally these are people who are torn
between two roles. The second generation immigrant is the
classic case. He has not yet accepted the values of his new

country nor discarded those of his old country. Similarly men and women who cannot accept their sex role, light-skinned Negroes who are sometimes taken for white, or anyone else who does not clearly fit into one position in society tends to be at least temporarily marginal. Although the notion of marginality is quite different from our conception of deviancy, there is much in common. The marginal man is one who is not integrated into any group and thus has no group which he is not to some extent deviant from. In this sense he is a deviant, albeit a very special kind. The very tall person while deviant is probably not marginal. But most marginal men would be considered deviants.

The emphasis in this work is on the behavior of these marginal men, and on possible solutions to their problems. As such it is fairly close to our interests, although the kinds of groups it involves are quite limited and specialized.

Finally, there are experimental studies involving either particular types of deviants that exist in society or experimentally induced deviancy. This latter work is obviously the closest to ours in methodology, but the conception of deviancy is actually markedly different. The experiments all manipulate deviancy by telling the subject that he holds a position or opinion different from everyone else's. Then the extent to which he changes his opinion and, in some cases, the way the others treat him, are measured. This has some of the same features as our experiments, but there is what we consider a crucial difference. In this earlier work the content of the deviancy is not only known (i.e., he is deviant because he disagrees on the given issue) but also the measures taken are directly related to that content. For example, a subject is made to believe that he disagrees with the group in his prediction of what union leaders would do in a labor management dispute and the measure of attitude change is then how much he changes his views on this topic. (Festinger, Gerard, Hymovitch, Kelley, & Raven, 1952). The same is true of the typical conformity study (Asch, 1951) in which the subject probably does feel quite deviant when everyone picks an answer different from the one he favors, but then the measure is simply how much he conforms to the group answer. This work is clearly relevant to our problems, but it does not say much about how a general feeling of deviancy will affect behavior that is not directly related to the cause of the deviancy, which is our major concern.

Despite important differences from our approach, much of this extensive literature is clearly relevant to our problems. We shall discuss particular studies throughout the book when they concern the behavior being investigated in the separate chapters. For the moment, we would like to see if any general comments on deviancy can be extracted from this large and impressive array of material. With this work serving as a background, let us now turn to the question of what the major concerns of deviants might be. In what way, by what process, through what motivational steps do feelings of deviancy affect a person's behavior?

In the first place, it seems from anecdotal evidence, research, and intuition that deviants must be concerned about being mistreated because of their deviancy. It is almost a commonplace that people are suspicious of and unkind to others who are different from them. This assumption appears explicitly or implicitly in much of the literature on deviancy. Almost all descriptions of particular deviant groups emphasize the difficulties and mistreatment the groups face because of their differentness. This is one of the bases of the scapegoat theory of prejudice (e.g., Allport, 1944), it runs through Goffman's writings (e.g., 1963), and it is given some support by experimental work such as the study by Schachter (1951) in which deviants are given only the poorest jobs in a group. This mistreatment of deviants is sometimes even incorporated explicitly into the laws as shown by the following example from the Municipal Code of the City of San Francisco: "It shall be unlawful for any person, who is diseased, maimed, mutilated or deformed as to be an unsightly or improper person, to be allowed in or on public streets, highways, thoroughfares or public places, to expose himself or herself, or his or her injury or deformity to public view." (Police Code, Section 23).

Whether or not deviants actually are treated worse than nondeviants is for the moment irrelevant. (We shall return to this question and present some evidence in Chapters 6 and 7.) What is important is that virtually everyone believes that deviancy leads to mistreatment. Given this belief, deviants must be worried about the kind of treatment they will receive at the hands of nondeviants. Thus one of the deviant's motivations should be to avoid or minimize possible mistreatment due to his differentness.

The other major concern which we expect the deviant to have centers around his feelings about himself. Although most people would probably not like to be exactly the same as everyone else, they would also not like to be too different. Exactly where differentness and individuality turns into deviancy will vary enormously for different people, situations, and dimensions. But at some point almost anyone will begin to feel deviant, and we assume he would rather not be deviant. The literature is less explicit on this point, but discussions of passing (e.g., Stonequist, 1937; Goffman, 1963; etc.) make it clear that there are strong pressures toward appearing nondeviant. These and other books (e.g., Rechy, 1963) further suggest that deviants, at least those with traits which are generally considered to be negative, would prefer to be nondeviants. If this is correct, the deviant will be motivated to minimize or reduce his feelings of deviancy—or to put it another way, to convince himself that he is not deviant.

These are the two general notions with which we started our research—deviants would try to avoid mistreatment by others and to minimize their own feelings of deviancy. It seems likely that deviants have other motivations which distinguish them from nondeviants, but for the moment these were the ones that were clearest to us. In any case, as mentioned earlier, the basic orientation of this work was empirical rather than theoretical. The important question was how these, or other motivations would affect the deviant's behavior. Therefore, these simple assumptions about the deviant's concerns served primarily as a background against which to consider the problem of how deviants would differ from nondeviants in specific situations. With these ideas in mind, we attempted to select those behaviors which seemed most likely to be affected by feelings of deviancy and to construct experiments to reveal these effects.

2

THE BASIC PARADIGM

Introduction

As we said in the previous chapter, our goal was to see how deviancy per se influences people's behavior. To do this it is necessary to eliminate or at least hold constant the effect of the particular dimension on which the person is deviant and also, probably just as crucial, to remove the negative or positive valence of the particular deviant attribute. Although it would have been interesting and perhaps significant, we could not simply study various types of deviants in society, because each type of deviancy carries with it a large assortment of specific values, effects, etc. Being Negro means one thing and produces one effect; being blind, another; being a genius, another; being a giant, another. Inherent in any given deviant attribute is the actual meaning of that attribute in this society. This meaning in most cases has enormous influence on the person's behavior and on other's treatment of the deviant.

Similarly, each attribute tends to be either positive or negative, with probably most being considered negative. For example, it is generally considered negative to be very short or ugly or deformed, and thus very short people, ugly people, and deformed people are treated in various unpleasant ways. But short people and ugly people are also clearly deviants, and this may affect how they are treated. In other words, while it is a fact of life that many deviant attributes are considered negative by society, the effect of this negativity is something different from and hopefully distinguishable from the effect of the deviancy itself. The same holds for deviants who happen to have a characteristic which is generally considered positive, such as great beauty or outstanding intelligence or strength. The strong man is obviously treated in a special way in many situations. People probably do not go out of their way to make fun of him or to anger him. They may also, however, treat him specially because he is a deviant. Once again, it is this latter effect we want to discover.

One approach would have been to investigate how various kinds of deviants are actually treated and how they behave, and then to try to see regularities across the various types. In this way we might discover those effects which are due to deviancy per se, rather than to the particular characteristics. However, this did not seem to be a fruitful approach for two reasons: (1) It is extremely difficult to assemble a wide variety of deviants in anything like a controlled environment; and (2) more important, we felt that the effect of the particular characteristic would, in most cases, tend to obscure the effects of the deviancy.

Therefore, we did not choose this line of investigation. Instead, we decided to investigate deviancy in the laboratory by experimentally producing a feeling of deviancy in such a way that the particular content of the deviancy was unknown and the positive or negative character of it was unspecified. That is, we attempted to make people feel deviant without telling them specifically in what way they were deviant and at the same time assuring them that their deviant characteristics were neither good nor bad, but simply there. By avoiding any specific contents we hoped to discover how deviancy per se affects behavior and to rule out contamination and confusion caused by particular attributes or any evaluation put on the deviant characteristic. Although we were probably not entirely successful in this endeavor, we feel that it is, at least, a beginning of a systematic, rigorous investigation of this problem.

We should point out that the ambiguity of the information given the subjects in this procedure may have aroused feelings of confusion and uncertainty which would have caused the subjects to seek information about their deviancy. This motivation to discover how they were deviant might under some circumstances have important effects on their behavior. We shall discuss this possibility in more detail in Chapter 3. For the moment let us note that we felt that any effects produced by feelings of uncertainty would tend to be relatively minor in most situations. In any case, if we were going to eliminate specific content, the information necessarily had to be ambiguous. We felt that the gain in precision from this elimination more than offset the problem of dealing with possible effects of uncertainty.

Method

The method depended upon finding a way of telling the subjects that they were different from most people of their age and sex and, in particular, different from the rest of the group that was present. In addition, this had to be done without telling them exactly how they were different because any specific content would introduce all of the confoundings that we were trying to avoid. At the same time it was essential to give subjects the impression that the dimension on which they were deviant was important or otherwise they probably would not care very much. We did not, for example, want to tell them that we had developed a new and esoteric test of liver activity and that their liver, while it was perfectly healthy, behaved quite differently from most people's. This kind of thing might make some people feel deviant, but we felt that most people would simply accept our statement and be entirely unconcerned and unmoved. Since one central assumption was that the person must *feel* deviant for it to affect him, we needed a dimension which would be salient enough and important enough to make the subject feel deviant.

With all of this in mind, we decided to use a manipulation involving the individual's "personality." We planned to tell subjects that we were testing their total personality, that we were trying to get a picture of "what they were like." No particular dimensons of personality were ever mentioned. Since "personality" is quite a vague but at the same time obviously very important concept, we were able to tell subjects "what they were like" without giving them any content, and without having any difficulty in making them believe us. The basic procedure was to give subjects very complex, impressive "personality" tests. Then, some of them were told that they were quite different from most people while others were told that they were quite similar to most people. Throughout this procedure the nonevaluative nature of the tests was stressed—we were simply trying to find out about the subjects, there were no right or wrong answers, and so on.

There were several variations of this procedure but the differences among them were relatively minor. Our standard method, which was used in most of the studies reported in his book, emerged after several experiments in which slightly different methods were used.

SUBJECTS

Subjects were recruited to take part in a psychology study. In most experiments they were paid $3.00 for approximately two hours of their time. In a few they were paid $2.00 or $2.50

for "less than an hour and a half." Different populations were used in the various experiments. College freshman males were recruited through notices posted in Stanford dormitories, directly by phone, or in person by someone other than the experimenter. High school girls were recruited directly by phone and also by ads placed in the local newspaper. In most experiments, appointments were confirmed by phone. In all studies, an attempt was made (not always successfully) to be certain that subjects in a particular group did not know each other. All experiments were run at Stanford University.

PROCEDURE

Subjects were run in groups of five or six, including the confederates if there were any. When they arrived they were told that they would be taking a personality test. The experimenter then seated the subjects, usually in one room, in separate booths which were constructed so that each subject could see forward but could not see any other subject. This separation was necessary because subjects were receiving different feedback sheets during the course of the test and it was essential that they did not know this. Each subject was then given a code letter (A—F) which was picked at random from a box.

The experimenter attempted to impress upon the subjects that the test they were going to take was an extremely reliable personality inventory that had been very well tested and validated and so on. He gave more or less standard personality test instructions to the effect that they should answer honestly and spontaneously, that there were no right or wrong answers, that what we wanted was their own feelings, reactions, and beliefs. He also said that the tests were completely confidential, but that subjects should put their names on them so that we could identify them. One point was stressed very strongly. This was

17

that the tests were entirely nonevaluative. They were designed to give us a picture of the individual taking them, to tell us what he was like. There was nothing negative or positive included in the scoring of the tests, there were no good or bad scores, there was only a description of the person.

It was then explained that the inventory consisted of a series of five personality tests and that they would be given feedback on their results after each one. All of the subjects' responses were on IBM cards to make it plausible that the tests could be scored quickly and accurately. Before they began the tests they were shown a sample feedback sheet which supposedly gave the results of a group that had taken the test a few weeks before. The purpose of this sheet was to aid in explaining how the feedback sheets worked. The sample showed five or six people who were nondeviant. The experimenter explained the meaning of the various scores and made it clear that the subjects could identify their own scores by their code letters.

The experimenter made certain that all subjects thoroughly understood the feedback sheet, and he then distributed the first test. When the subjects had completed this test, the experimenter collected the test forms and answer cards, and handed out the second test. While subjects were working on it, the experimenter was supposedly scoring the first test. When the second test was finished, subjects were given their results on the first plus the forms for the third and so on through the last test. After the last test, subjects sat and waited (without talking) while the experimenter supposedly finished scoring the last test and prepared the "summary" sheet. This summary was described to the subjects as "a composite of the rest of the tests. It is obviously not just an arithmetic mean or average of the rest. It is a general overview of the whole thing drawn from questions on all five tests that you took."

To summarize: The subjects took five tests. After the second, they received feedback on the first; after the third, feedback on the second; etc. Immediately after the fifth test, they received feedback on the fourth. Then a few minutes later, they were given feedback on the fifth plus a summary sheet of all tests.

THE TESTS

The personality inventory consisted of five subtests. All of them were based on standard personality tests, but all but one (the Social Desirability Scale) were constructed especially for these experiments. The choice of tests was based on three major considerations: (1) They should be of the multiple-choice form so that they could be answered on an IBM card and presumably scored quickly; (2) they should at least give the appearance of dealing with complex, profound aspects of personality; and (3) they should be ambiguous enough so that the subject could not know what, if anything, he was revealing and would therefore believe the feedback he received. One test, the adjective check list, was also chosen because it enabled us to include a check on the deviancy manipulation. The tests were:

1. A variant of the Thematic Apperception Test (TAT). Subjects were given a booklet containing pictures each of which was followed by three multiple choice questions. The subject was required to select the alternative that most clearly described his perception of the picture.

2. Edwards Personal Preference Inventory. This consisted of 12 items from the standard test. The subject indicated which of the two statements best described him. We selected items in which the alternatives seemed particularly evenly matched.

3. A variant of the Rorschach. This was similar to the TAT described above, except that Rorschach pictures were used.

19

4. The Marlowe-Crowne Social Desirability Scale. Standard form.

5. Self-description. Subjects indicated where they fell on each of seven dimensions defined by polar adjectives (e.g., good-bad). One of the dimensions was "similar-different" which was included as a check on the deviancy manipulation.

Thematic apperception test

Score	% receiving this score
0 - 5	1
6 - 9	2
10 - 12	2
13 - 15	10
16 - 20	29
21 - 24	25
25 - 27	18
28 - 30	8
31 - 33	3
34 - 40	2

Person	Score
A	25
B	3
C	22
D	24
E	23

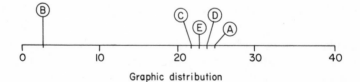

Graphic distribution

FIGURE 1. Feedback for the deviant subject.

Thematic apperception test

Score	% receiving this score
0 - 5	1
6 - 9	2
10 - 12	2
13 - 15	10
16 - 20	29
21 - 24	25
25 - 27	18
28 - 30	8
31 - 33	3
34 - 40	2

Person	Score
A	25
B	24
C	21
D	22
E	23

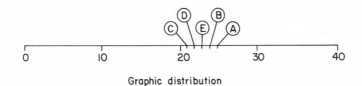

Graphic distribution

FIGURE 2. Feedback for the nondeviant subject.

FEEDBACK SHEETS

Since the manipulation of deviancy depended upon the feedback which the subjects were given, the construction of the feedback sheets was quite critical. Sample deviant and nondeviant feedback sheets are shown in Figures 1 and 2.

21

Subjects in the "deviant" conditions received scores at or near the end of the distribution on each of the six scales. The scores were at one end of some scales and the opposite end of others in order to control for any effect of the direction of the deviancy. In addition, which end was used for any given scale was counterbalanced among the deviants (e.g., some deviants were given scores at the "low" end of Scale 1 and "high" end of Scale 2, while others received scores at the "high" end of 1 and the "low" end of 2). Among the six deviant scores, only two were at the very end of the disbribution, with the rest ranging from second from the end to somewhat less extreme. This was done to make the scores more credible.

In contrast, subjects in the "nondeviant" condition received scores at or near the middle of the distribution. Since being completely "average" might have appeared implausible or unpleasant, each nondeviant was given one or two slightly deviant scores (i.e., about one standard deviation from the mean); but the summary scale and the overall impression were definitely nondeviant.

The deviancy manipulation was followed by a variety of procedures depending upon the particular concern of the experiment. These will be described in the appropriate chapters. At the conclusion of the study the experimenter spent a considerable amount of time explaining to the subjects what the study had been about. The most important point was, of course, that the feedback from the personality tests was false. He explained this in great detail, went over it again and again until it was certain that everyone understood, and answered any questions that the subject might have. It should be noted that in many cases the subjects required some convincing since apparently the original manipulation was both believable and impressive. However, all subjects were clear about this point by the time they left the experiment.

We also feel that no subject was appreciably upset by the manipulation. It was believable and powerful, and they did feel somewhat deviant for a while. However, probably because it lacked any content, it did not bother them as much as a seemingly less basic manipulation might have. Many "deviant" subjects probably found the information unpleasant and would have preferred to be nondeviants; but this effect was neither profound nor lasting. The explanation at the end of the study appeared to be sufficient to remove whatever effect the manipulation had had.

Checks on the Manipulation

As with any such manipulation, it is nice to have some direct check to assess whether or not and how well it worked. Such checks are reassuring if they are positive, even though they are far from definitive evidence. The problem is that in most cases, and in our case in particular, it is difficult to design a really good check. What we want to do is ask the subject how deviant he feels, but we want to do this in such a way that we are sure that he means the same thing as we do by the term "deviant" and we also want to be sure that his answer is trustworthy. Both of those criteria for a good check are difficult to provide. Since we tend to have little faith in these types of checks, and because extensive questioning of subjects convinced us that the manipulation was having the desired effect, we decided to use a question which quite directly asked S how deviant he felt. Although it is possible to be skeptical of results based on such a transparent question and to worry about demand characteristics of the situation and other such factors, for want of a better check we settled on this straightforward one.

One item of the semantic-differential type self-rating test was marked "similar" at one end and "different" at the other. Thus, the subject was presumably telling us how similar or different he was; we assumed that by this he was comparing himself to whatever reference group was most salient for him. The results of this check were consistent across all of our experiments. In all instances the experimentally manipulated deviant group rated themselves more "different" than did the nondeviant group. The strength of the effect varied from experiment to experiment, but was always fairly sizable. The range of significance levels was .01 to only marginally significant .10, with most experiments producing significant differences. Thus, this item indicates that the manipulation of deviancy was generally successful and, at least on the basis of this question, was often very strong. It should be noted that even though this item appeared in the last test, the subject had received only about half of the feedback since he had not yet seen his scores on the fourth and fifth tests or the summary sheet. Presumably, the effects would be strengthened by these other deviant scores. The fact that even this rather simple-minded question, given before the manipulation was completed, produced differences between groups is quite encouraging.

Several of the experiments also included other questions designed to check feelings of deviancy. Subjects were asked in several cases "How different do you feel from most people of your age and sex?" They responded on an undivided scale marked "Extremely different" and "Very similar" at the two ends. Once again, the deviant subjects rated themselves significantly more different than did the nondeviant subjects.

In one experiment subjects were asked "Do you think you are different from most of the people around you?" and if yes, how different. The first part was answered simply "yes" or "no" while the second part was answered on an unmarked scale.

Practically all subjects responded yes, but the deviants rated themselves significantly more different than did the non-deviants.

Thus, all of the direct checks on the manipulation were in the expected direction — the subjects who had received deviant feedback rated themselves more deviant than did those who had received nondeviant scores. In contrast, the groups did not differ appreciably on other self-description items (e.g., honest-dishonest, good-bad, strong-weak, likable-nonlikable etc.). It appears that the manipulation made them feel deviant but did not generally lower their self-esteem or change their estimates of other personality dimensions.

Similar findings appear in those studies in which we attempted to make the subjects think someone else in the group was either a deviant or a nondeviant. In all cases, when asked to rate these individuals, subjects rated the "deviant" more deviant than they rated the "nondeviant." In other words, the manipulation worked not only on the subject himself but also on his perception of particular other subjects.

All of this, then, seems to suggest that our manipulation of deviancy was effective. Manipulation checks of this kind are not, of course, unequivocal evidence that the manipulation worked, but they are at least encouraging. In Chapter 5 we shall present other kinds of evidence which is more supportive of our interpretation of the manipulation, but for the moment it is sufficient to say that the manipulation checks were in line with our expectations.

3

AFFILIATION

Introduction

One of our basic hypotheses about deviancy is that it greatly increases the individual's concern about being mistreated by others. If deviancy is perceived as negative in some sense, there always exists the possibility that the deviant will be rejected by nondeviants or mistreated in some other way. Whether or not this, in fact, happened, or would happen in a particular situation is essentially irrelevant—the critical factor is that the deviant himself will be worried about this possibility. Of course, it is extremely likely that the nature of the particular dimension on which the individual is deviant will exacerbate or diminish this fear, depending upon how negative this type of deviancy is generally thought to be and how negatively it is treated. But it is our assumption that this same concern exists for all deviants regardless of the nature of their own special kind of deviancy. Just as a homosexual may be rejected by a group of heterosexuals, so might a genius be rejected by a group of nongeniuses. The homosexual may be subjected to more abuse, but the genius will also be left out of the group and perhaps even abused. At least this fear will be shared by both. And this concern that his deviancy will cause others to treat him less well than if he were not deviant is an important determinant of the deviant's behavior.

If all of this is correct, the deviant should act so as to minimize the likelihood of being mistreated because of his deviancy. With this in mind, he should attempt various kinds of defensive maneuvers in his relations with other people. One of the most obvious and effective procedures would be to avoid contact with people who are likely to mistreat him and to seek out those who will treat him well. Whenever he can, he should, other things being equal, prefer to affiliate with someone to whom his deviancy is likely to be acceptable or at least who will tend not to reject him because of it. In other words, when he is able to choose whom to associate with, one of his primary considerations should be how the other person is likely to feel about deviants.

Given this proposition, it may readily be seen that deviants should prefer to associate with deviants who are like themselves rather than with nondeviants (i.e., even disregarding all of the other reasons for this being true). Presumably these other deviants, since they share his peculiarity, should be relatively accepting of it and will tend not to persecute or reject him because of this deviant characteristic.

Another, though less likely possibility, is that deviants should also prefer the company of deviants who are different from them to that of nondeviants. The rationale for this depends on the notion that all deviants have in common the fact of their deviancy and that to some extent two deviants, even if they are different from each other, are more similar than are a deviant and a nondeviant. If this is true, someone who is deviant himself should tend to be more accepting of deviancy in others than would a nondeviant. It would follow from this that deviants would expect better treatment at the hands of a different deviant than from a nondeviant, and that they would accordingly choose the former over the latter. Once again note that the critical consideration here is the deviant's perception of how the other will act, not how the other actually acts (except, of course, in the long run in so far as it influences that perception).

Thus, based on a few general ideas about deviancy we are led to two expectations about their affiliative preferences: (1) Deviants should prefer to affiliate with other, similar deviants rather than with nondeviants; and (2) there is some possibility that this will hold even for deviants who are different from those making the choice.

The psychological literature offers at least one other principle which might make similar predictions. The theory of social comparison (Festinger, 1954) proposes that people have a need to compare themselves to others, and that for this comparison they tend to prefer people who are similar to them. According to the theory, the reason for this preference is that comparing oneself to someone who is quite different does not provide the information which is sought. The person wants to evaluate his abilities, values, emotions, etc. He wants to find out how good he is in terms of his abilities and how appropriate and accurate his values and emotions are. The high school violinist does not gain much from comparing himself to Heifitz — true he is not as good as Heifitz, but the difference between them is so immense that the boy has learned essentially nothing about his own abilities. Comparison with another high school violinist will tell him much more since they will presumably be fairly close in ability and he can see if he is better, worse, or about equal. In addition, even if their musical technique is very disparate, knowing that he is much worse than another high school boy tells him a great deal more than the knowledge that he is much worse than Heifitz.

Similar arguments hold for values and emotions. The ethical standards of a lower class Chinese peasant are a poor reference point for an upper class French aristocrat. Neither the Chinese nor the Frenchman would learn much about himself by knowing the other's values. The student who is studying for an exam may want to find out how nervous he should be. Comparing himself to the teacher will not help — unfortunately the teacher is giving, not taking the exam. In fact, comparing himself to a student who is much poorer or much smarter will not help much either. What the student needs is to compare himself to someone who is similar to him in ability. The theory, therefore, predicts that for purposes of social comparison people will tend to affiliate with others who are similar to them. A number of studies have supported this prediction (Schachter, 1959; Darley & Aronson, 1966; Hakmiller, 1966; Zimbardo & Formica, 1963; etc.).

This should also hold for deviants. To the extent that they are motivated to find out about themselves or about how they should behave, deviants should want to affiiliate with people who are similar to them. As we mentioned earlier, our manipulation of deviancy produces considerable uncertainty and these needs for social comparison should accordingly be quite strong. Therefore, deviants should clearly prefer similar deviants to nondeviants.

The expectation regarding different deviants is less clear. On the one hand, the deviant might be primarily concerned about how his particular type of deviancy should affect his behavior, or about how he could behave so as to minimize his deviancy. In either case, the nondeviant who is, after all, closer on the critical dimension than is the different deviant, would be a better source of information. This would, of course, produce a preference for nondeviants over different deviants.

On the other hand, it seems to us equally plausible that deviants want to find out about themselves, and particularly in our studies about how and why they are deviant. Since the different deviant is at the opposite end of the continuum, his deviant characteristic should be quite noticeable and the subject could accordingly discover at least the dimension on which he deviates. In addition, affiliating with a different deviant might enable a deviant to learn how deviants in general are supposed to behave in society. A nondeviant would be a relatively poor source of information about either the source of the subject's deviancy or about suitable behavior for deviants. This rationale would make us expect deviants to prefer different deviants to nondeviants.

Reasoning in terms of either fear of rejection or social comparison, therefore, leads to the clear expectation that deviants will affiliate with similar deviants rather than with nondeviants, but only suggests that deviants may also prefer different deviants to nondeviants. Either fear of rejection or needs for social comparison could produce these effects. In fact, it seems likely that other theories could be found or constructed which would make similar predictions. This conceptual underpinning has, however, been provided primarily as a rationale for investigating this phenomenon rather than as a theoretical position to be tested. Let us turn then to a consideration of the relevant literature to see if there is anything to indicate that deviancy does indeed have the effects we have described.

There is a great deal of anecdotal evidence consistent with these expectations. It appears that deviants in society do tend to associate with one another. Artists tend to associate with artists, communists with communists, Jews with Jews, little people with little people (there is an association of little people), and so on. Furthermore, to some extent deviants associate with other deviants who are different from them more than they do with nondeviants. Various kinds of sexual deviants, artists, musicians, and addicts seem to prefer each other's company to that of more "average" individuals, even when the two kinds of deviants are very different from each other.

This phenomenon is particularly noticeable in those areas of large cities which are the meeting places of these groups. Greenwich Village in New York is probably the most famous spot of this kind, but there are equivalent areas in virtually every large city as well as many smaller cities. This pattern of association may not include all kinds of deviants and there may be certain subsets of deviants that associate with each other but not with other subsets; but it seems clear that to an important extent deviants do affiliate more with other deviants than they do with nondeviants.

A rather extreme example of this tendency occurred in California recently. There are two well-known groups called "Hell's Angels" and "The Hippies." The former is a motorcycle group that has been associated with some right wing causes. Its members have often sported Nazi armbands and have been accused of various violent acts such as trying to break up a war protest rally, terrorizing towns, gang rapes, and so on. The latter, a relatively new and unorganized group, is much less political, but is if anything somewhat left wing. Its members are associated with peace rallies, favor long hair, rock-and-roll and especially folk-rock, advocate the use of LSD, and are generally liberal. Both groups are clearly deviant from the surrounding society. In 1965, the Hell's Angels attempted to disrupt a Hippie rally by running their motorcycles through the center of it.

In 1966, however, everything changed and the two groups became, at least publicly, closely affiliated. The Hell's Angels actually took part in the Hippie rally and to some extent served as protectors of it from other gangs (San Francisco Chronicle, January 2, 1967). According to newspaper reports associations between the two groups are close and friendly now. In other

31

words, despite their marked differences the two deviant groups have ended up affiliating with each other.

There are practical reasons for deviants to spend their time with other similar deviants. They may do this because only the other deviants can supply certain things that they need. Homosexuals need other homosexuals to satisfy their sexual needs, dope addicts can get dope from other addicts (or at least around other addicts), painters and musicians presumably get stimulation, advice, and jobs from other painters and musicians, and so on.

Deviants also tend to share certain values and attitudes, and these may draw them together. The musicians may, for example, like to attend jazz recitals while most squares would not—so musicians would naturally go to this particular activity together. Similarly, Jews attend synagogue while Protestants do not; communists must occasionally attend cell meetings or talks by radical speakers; and so on. These are very trivial examples and it would be easy to multiply them almost indefinitely. Sharing particular values and interests will draw people together; and, of course, deviants of similar or related types will tend to have common values.

None of this explains why deviants of quite different types would tend to prefer each other's company to that of nondeviants, but there are various forces in society which must, to some extent, be responsible for this.

Perhaps the most powerful force producing this congregation is the police. Men responsible for law enforcement in a community are faced with a difficult problem in dealing with certain kinds of deviants. Some, such as sexual deviants or dope addicts, are to some extent outlawed by statute. It is usually illegal to dress in clothes appropriate to the opposite sex; it is always illegal to solicit for homosexual or perverse sexual practices; and possession of any narcotic without a doctor's prescription is a serious offense. Other types of deviants, while not controlled by statute, are considered undesirable by the local mores. Artists with or without beards are suspect even when they are financially successful; the same is true of musicians, unusual religious sects, political radicals, etc. Policemen have the task of controlling many of these elements of society as well as some power with which to carry out this task.

What this means in practice is that the police force finds it necessary to tolerate these undesirable types of deviants but does so only on certain terms. Usually the terms are that the deviants confine themselves to a certain area of the city, avoid "bothering" nondeviants, and in general be as unobtrusive as possible whenever they stray from their territory. In other words, to avoid prosecution or persecution from the law the deviants must remain in a small area (Smith, 1960, pp. 18, 19). Since this area is often the same for all kinds of deviants, they are automatically thrown together and tend to associate with each other. Similar pressures are brought to bear by restrictive housing for Negroes and sometimes Jews, cost of housing for struggling artists, noise restrictions for musicians, and so on. Thus, a variety of social forces and practical considerations push both similar and different deviants together.

It appears that in society deviants do tend to associate with other deviants. However, since there are many extraneous reasons for this, it would be highly desirable to see whether this pattern of affiliative preferences holds in more controlled situations in which external pressures are eliminated (or at least held constant) and in which the specific nature of the deviancy is relatively ambiguous or unimportant. If the pattern appears under these conditions, it would suggest that the feeling of deviancy itself was producing the preferences and would constitute some support for our previous discussion in terms of fear of rejection or social comparison.

A laboratory experiment was conducted to test the hypothesis that, other things being equal, deviants who are given a choice of affiliating with deviants like themselves (similar deviants), deviants unlike themselves (different deviants), or nondeviants would choose more similar deviants than would nondeviants given a similar choice; and furthermore this may hold for different deviants.

Choice of Partners

Subjects were made to feel either deviant or nondeviant by the use of a variation of the manipulation described in detail in Chapter 2 and were then given a choice of affiliating with deviants at either end of a personality dimension or with nondeviants. The primary data for our present purpose are the subject's preferences among these other individuals.

METHOD

Subjects were 47 male freshmen at Stanford University (as explained below, 54 began the study but only 47 completed it). They had taken part in no psychology experiments and had taken no psychology classes. They were recruited by letter and were paid $3.00 for two 1-hour sessions. The first session was run in groups of from six to fifteen. It consisted entirely of taking the personality inventory which is described in Chapter 2. Subjects were told that everything would be explained at the second session, that for the purposes of keeping the experiment controlled (with a lengthy explanation) it was essential that they not talk about the test with anyone until the whole study was completed, and finally that they would be contacted within a few weeks to set up a time for the second session. This first session took approximately one hour.

The second session took place about two weeks later. All subjects who had taken part in the first session were contacted by phone and asked to come to the second session. Seven subjects did not attend the second session of the study. The remaining 47 were run in groups ranging in size from three to six (with all but a few being five or six).

The subjects in each group were seated around a table. It was explained in all cases that six subjects had been scheduled for this time but that (when appropriate) apparently not all were going to show up. The subjects were then handed a booklet containing a variety of materials. Stapled to the back of the booklet was a sheet described as a summary of the results of the personality test. This sheet supposedly contained the scores of all subjects who had taken the test. In fact, 62 scores were indicated by code number on each of the five scales. Six scores, supposedly belonging to the members of the present group, were circled. Twenty-four of these summary sheets had one circled number which was consistently deviant, with the other five numbers being at or near the middle of the distribution; 23 had all six numbers in the middle. The deviant score was placed at or near the end of some scales and at the opposite end of others. This was to avoid as much as possible the attribution of a negative or positive value to the direction of deviance, and this was reinforced by the instructions quoted previously to the effect that the scales were nonevaluative, etc.

The procedure also included a manipulation of whether or not the subject thought his scores were public knowledge. In the unknown condition (i.e., scores were confidential) the subject's code number was written on his test booklet. Only he could see it and it was never mentioned publicly. Since it was impossible for any of the other subjects to know this number, they could not match him with his scores on the test summary. Thus, if he were deviant, the other subjects would presumably know only that there was a deviant in the group but would not know who he was. In the known condition (i.e., the scores were public knowledge) the code numbers were not on the booklets. Instead the experimenter read them aloud. He read each subject's name and code number slowly and then asked each subject to repeat his number presumably to be certain that everyone had the correct number. In this way each person was clearly associated with a particular code number; and it must have appeared very likely that everyone would notice who had the deviant scores. In fact, it should be remembered that only the deviants had summary sheets on which there were deviant scores, and in all cases it was their scores that were deviant. The nondeviants saw the group as consisting of six quite nondeviant individuals; the deviants saw the group as consisting of five nondeviants plus themselves.

After the subjects had had about ten minutes to look over the summary sheets, the experimenter explained that he would go into more detail about the meaning of the various scales when the study was completed. He then instructed the subjects to open the test booklet and proceed with the tests. The subjects went through a variety of procedures designed in part to increase the power and salience of the deviancy manipulation and in part to test several other hypotheses about reactions to a feeling of deviancy. These other hypotheses will be discussed in a later chapter. The main point for our present purpose is that during these tests the subjects were made to think often about their own and others' personalities, to compare themselves to the rest of the subjects, and in general to think about how they stood vis à vis the group.

The Choice

The test booklet was completed in about 25 minutes. The study was presumably over and at this point the experimenter, in what was supposed to be a rather offhand way, said he had been asked to help out a fellow experimenter. This other experimenter, it was explained, was running a study on cooperative problem solving. He was trying to set up two-man teams to work on problems, and he was going to pay very well for taking part in the study. One of the things he was interested in studying was the relationship of personality and performance and he had, therefore, given a number of sophomores part of the same personality test the present subjects had taken. He wanted to pair each of these sophomores with a freshman, had heard that subjects in this study had also taken the test, and thought they would be ideal for his study.

Furthermore, he would like to give subjects some choice of partners and had decided to do this by showing the freshmen the sophomores' scores on the personality test and letting them choose on the basis of these scores. The experimenter then said that, of course, the subjects knew very little about what these scores meant and that the other experimenter knew this but that this was the way he wanted it done. The subjects were urged to go along with the procedure, look at the scores of the other sample of subjects, and pick out those three subjects they would most like to work with. It was explained that it was not certain that they would be called to take part—some would be chosen purely at random—but they were all asked to give their choices.

They were then handed a sheet identical to the summary sheet they already had except that only the last scale was marked, and only 25 numbers were written in. Note that the subjects themselves still had their own summary sheets in front of them (which they immediately consulted). The deviant subjects had a score second from the bottom on this last scale while the nondeviants were right in the middle. Although all of this may seem rather complicated, the subjects, in fact, took it seemingly in their stride and dutifully marked down the numbers of the three sophomores they most preferred as partners. This ended the experiment.

RESULTS

Deviants vs. Non deviants

To begin with, we may look at the choices without distinguishing between similar and different deviants. The simplest way of looking at the data is in terms of the total number of deviant choices made by each group with deviant choices being defined as the three top and bottom scores. This definition is not as arbitrary as it may sound since these six scores do stand out to some extent from the rest. Table 3.1 presents the number of extreme and nonextreme choices defined in this way. It is evident that the deviants chose considerably more deviants than did the nondeviants. The difference is highly significant $(t = 3.24, p < .01)$.

TABLE 3.1
AFFILIATIVE CHOICES

Subjects		Number of deviants chosen	Weighted deviancy score
Deviant	$(24)^a$	2.00	7.29
Nondeviant	(23)	0.91	3.78

^{a}Figure in parentheses is number in the group.

A somewhat more sensitive measure of this same preference may be obtained by giving each choice a weighted extremity or deviancy score. Choosing the most extreme score may indicate a greater preference for a deviant than choosing the third most extreme; and choosing the fifth or even the seventh may still show more preference for deviancy than choosing the median score. To measure this the scores were divided into five groups and assigned weights: top and bottom score, 4; next two, 3; next two, 2; next three, 1; and the rest, 0. These are fairly natural groupings.

The results of this scoring method are also presented in Table 3.1. A score of 0 indicates a choice of three scores right at the median, while a score of 11 is the maximum deviancy score indicating a choice of both most extreme scores and the one next most extreme. Once again the difference between groups is as predicted. The deviants have a much greater tendency to choose extreme individuals than do the nondeviants, and the difference is highly significant. ($t = 3.55$, $p < .01$).

A somewhat different question is whether or not the deviants actually choose more deviants than would be expected by chance. There are 25 scores to choose from and only six really deviant scores. A completely random choice of three scores would be expected to include .72 of these six deviant scores. The deviant subjects actually averaged 2.00 extreme choices which is significantly different from what would be expected by chance ($t = 4.83$, $p < .001$).

The nondeviant group also chose slightly more than the chance number of extreme scores (.91 vs. .72) but this difference is not significant ($t < 1.0$). In other words, whereas the nondeviants select about as many deviants as might be expected if the choice were random, the deviant subjects show a clear preference for affiliating with deviants rather than with nondeviants.

It should be remembered, however, that this analysis is based

39

on the assumption of random choices. In fact, it seems unlikely that any subjects would consider the 25 scores equally attractive or equally choosable. The middle scores and the end scores probably tend to stand out in some way and would probably be picked more often than other scores just as a person who is asked to pick a card, any card, tends either to pick one that is thrust forward a little or one that is clearly held back. The analogy is loose, but the same kind of selection probably does go on. This means that we have no way of knowing if the deviants were deliberately picking deviants or if the nondeviants were, in fact, deliberately avoiding deviants. For the moment we shall assume that the deviants were trying to pick deviants but shall hold open the possibility that the nondeviants were also seeking out nondeviants or avoiding deviants. Hopefully additional research will clarify this point.

Similar vs. Different Deviants

The next question is how these preferences are affected by whether the other deviants are similar or different. In the present situation the subject had a choice of deviants at both ends of a personality scale. It should be remembered that the experimenter repeatedly stressed that the scales were nonevaluative and that the top and bottom did not in any way indicate the good and bad ends of the continuum. The two ends of the scale did, however, indicate very different personality characteristics. Since the deviant subjects were at the bottom of this particular scale, the other deviants who had low scores must have appeared similar to them while those with high scores appeared different from the deviant subjects. The choices may thus be broken down into deviants above the median and deviants below the median which would correspond to dissimilar and similar deviants, respectively. These results in terms of both number of deviant choices and weighted scores are presented in Tables 3.2 and 3.3.

TABLE 3.2
MEAN NUMBER OF DEVIANTS CHOSEN

Subjects	Above median (different deviants)	Below median (similar deviants)
Deviant	1.21	0.79
Nondeviant	0.52	0.39

TABLE 3.3
WEIGHTED MEAN OF DEVIANTS CHOSEN

Subjects	Above median (different deviants)	Below median (similar deviants)
Deviant	4.04	3.25
Nondeviant	2.08	1.70

The important comparisons for our hypotheses are between deviants and nondeviants. The deviant makes more deviant choices than does the nondeviant both above and below the median. The difference between the two groups is significant for above median choices ($t = 2.45$, $p < .05$) and almost significant for below median choices ($t = 1.87$, $p < .10$) when computed on simple number of deviants chosen. Using the weighted scores, which are somewhat more sensitive, both differences reach acceptable levels of significance ($t = 2.24$, $p < .05$ and 2.10, $p < .05$, respectively). In other words, not only do deviants prefer to associate with other deviants, but this preference holds even when the other deviants are presumably very different from them.

41

It should be noted that the differentness in this situation is on the same dimension. The different deviants are not different in some entirely unrelated way—rather they are at the opposite end of the dimension on which the subject is deviant. This, of course, assumes that they are extremely different in some sense. On the other hand, it may conceivably be that differentness along an unrelated dimension would not produce the same pattern of results. Perhaps deviants would not choose to affiliate with people who are deviant along some other dimensions. We have no data relevant to this, but it does seem somewhat unlikely, at least in the present context.

Known vs. Unknown

Some of the subjects were known deviants and some were unknown. They were all choosing someone who might be their working partner. Under these circumstances, we did not expect the visibility of their deviancy to make much difference in their preference for deviants over nondeviants. The unknown deviants might be a little less concerned about being mistreated because their deviancy would not be public knowledge, but they should still prefer someone who, if he did discover that they were deviant, would be accepting. In addition, there was some ambiguity about whether this other person would know their scores on the test, even when the scores were known to the group. We thus expected that both known and unknown deviants would prefer to associate with other deviants and that there would be little difference between the two groups in these preferences. This is what was found. For both total and weighted choices known and unknown deviants strongly preferred to work with other deviants, and there was no appreciable difference between the two groups.

A minor point that may be of some interest is that there is a slight tendency for all groups to choose more deviants above the median than below. None of the differences between above and below approach significance but it may be suggestive evidence that despite all our instructions to the contrary, the top of the scale still tended to be seen as the "good" end by many subjects. Or, it may be due simply to the fact that the eye tends to be drawn to the top scores. In any case, this slight trend did exist. In all future studies horizontal scales rather than vertical scales were used, and deviant subjects were carefully placed sometimes at one end and sometimes at the other.

In this study freshmen subjects were making choices among sophomores with whom they might end up working. The choices were thus more or less hypothetical. In addition, they were made on the basis of only one scale on the personality test which may have made the information somewhat non-comparable to what the subject was given himself. Despite these aspects of the experiment, we obtained the results we predicted. Nevertheless, it seemed desirable to replicate the study with the choices being more realistic and the personality information about the other people more complete.

Replication

METHOD

Subjects were 20 high school girls who were paid $2.50 for taking part in the experiment. They were made to believe that there were six other subjects in another room which was, in fact, true since these other subjects were being run as part of a different experiment. The subject received feedback on seven subjects including herself.

43

When the personality test was completed, the subject was handed a sheet containing the choice instructions. It was explained that the second part of the study (which was going to be run right then) consisted of two-person teams working on problems. The subject was asked to indicate her preferences for team member among the six other subjects by ranking the three she would most like to work with. For all subjects the pattern of scores for the other six "subjects" was identical. Four of them were clearly nondeviant with scores at or near the middle of the distribution of all scales; two were deviant. One of the deviants had scores very similar to that of the deviant subject; one had essentially opposite scores (similar and different deviants). Thus, all subjects were choosing among four nondeviants and two deviants; and for deviant subjects, one of the deviants was similar to her and the other was different.

RESULTS

The results may be scored most simply in terms of the rank given to the two deviants with first scored as three, second place as two, and third as one. Since there were two deviants and three choices, the maximum score was 5 (i.e., deviants chosen first and second) and the minimum was 0 (no deviants chosen). The means for deviant and nondeviant subjects are quite different. The deviants average 4.4 (just slightly less than maximum) while the nondeviants averaged 2.99. The t for the difference between the experimental groups is 1.99, $p < .06$. In contrast to the first study, however, this effect holds only for similar deviants. Although deviant subjects choose different deviants slightly more than do nondeviants, this difference does not approach significance. Thus, these results clearly replicate the earlier finding that similar deviants are preferred, but do not show the previous preference for different deviants.

As noted above, in the first study "different" deviants were always at the top of the scale and "similar" deviants at the bottom. In that study different deviants were chosen somewhat more than similar, particularly by unknown deviant subjects. In the replication the position of the deviants was systematically varied and the scales ran horizontally rather than vertically, thus probably looking less evaluative. Also, all deviants were essentially known since their letter stood out. Under these conditions there was a significant tendency for deviants to choose more similar than different deviants ($t = 2.53, p < .05$). This preference for similar deviants makes good sense in terms of our original assumptions about the underlying motivation. Known deviants should be trying to maximize the likelihood of being accepted (or not rejected) and should naturally not be concerned with concealing their deviancy because it is already known. Since similar deviants should be a better bet than different deviants and would be most likely to be accepting of these deviant subjects, the former should be preferred.

To summarize, the main finding in this study is that with the choice being more meaningful, the information more complete, and the affiliation more imminent, one result of the first study is replicated but another is not. Deviants do show a preference for similar deviants, but this preference does not extend to different deviants.

Just why this latter result failed to replicate is unclear. The studies differed in a number of ways, some of which have been mentioned above, but there is no particular reason to expect any of these relatively minor differences to produce this major change in the deviants' preferences. For the moment we are left with no explanation. It appears that we may be quite confident that deviants do prefer other similar deviants; but whether or not they also prefer different deviants is uncertain.

It should be noted that in these two studies the subjects knew nothing about the other people except their scores on the personality inventory. Since this was the only information available, it was natural for the affiliation choices to be maximally influenced by these scores. Under these rarefied circumstances, the deviancy of the other individual was very important. We saw that, other things being equal, deviants prefer to affiliate with other deviants. Other things are, of course, not always equal. People usually know more about other people than simply whether or not they are deviant. When they have this additional information, it seems unlikely that deviancy will make as large a difference as it did in the situations studied here. In other words, the very strong effect of deviancy found in these experiments should be considered with the knowledge that we were studying quite unusual situations. The results should not be interpreted as indicating that deviancy is the major factor determining choice of associates. On the other hand, the findings do seem to indicate that deviancy is *one* important factor and that particularly when little other information is available it may be the critical determinant of whom someone chooses to affiliate with.

Summary and Discussion

We have seen that deviant subjects tend to prefer associating with other deviants more than do nondeviants and that this may be true even for other deviants who are unlike themselves. How do these findings fit in with our previous suggestions as to the underlying motivation produced by feelings of deviancy?

It seems evident that all of these results are consistent with explanations in terms of either fear of rejection or social comparison, as long as it is also assumed that being deviant is an important characteristic when attributed to any individual. As we described in detail at the beginning of this chapter, both fear of rejection and social comparison would tend to cause the deviants to prefer associating with other deviants who are similar to them. The possibility that they prefer deviants who are different from them to nondeviants is consistent with an analysis in terms of fear of rejection and can be fitted into the social comparison explanation although perhaps somewhat less easily. In other words, the major results are in the expected direction and provide some support for our analysis of the effect of deviancy on affiliation.

These two explanations are not, however, presented as an exhaustive list of the possible motives aroused by feelings of deviancy. It seems very likely that both of them as well as various others are operating to produce these results. Rather, as mentioned in Chapter 1, we are using these explanations as heuristic devices to help us concentrate on our major problem which is specifying what effects feelings of deviancy have on the deviant's behavior.

4

CONCEALMENT
OF DEVIANCY

Introduction

In the previous chapter we saw that when deviants were given a choice of whom to affiliate with they preferred other deviants to nondeviants. One possible explanation of this finding is that the deviant is protecting himself from possible mistreatment by choosing others who are most likely to be accepting of his deviancy. If the deviant is motivated by a feeling that he has to protect himself, he should also use various other defensive measures which may have significant effects on his behavior.

One very effective defense would be concealment of the deviancy. If the deviant can prevent others from knowing that he is different, he can obviously guarantee that he will not be mistreated because of his deviancy. Thus, other things being equal, when it is practicable there should be a tendency for deviants to attempt to hide their deviancy.

It is important to note, however, that the likelihood of concealment being successful differs greatly for different types of deviancy. Once the person is known to be deviant, of course, concealment, at least in that situation, is no longer possible. For certain kinds of deviants, their deviant characteristic is almost always immediately apparent. The eight foot giant, the three foot midget, the blind, the dark Negro, the paraplegic, and the grossly deformed cannot, under most circumstances, hope to conceal their deviancy. They are what Goffman (1963) labels "visible deviants." In addition, many who have non-visible deviant characteristics may nevertheless be known to be deviant and will thus be in the same situation as these "visible" deviants. Both "visible" and otherwise "known" deviants can try to minimize the extent of their differentness, but they cannot conceal that they are different.

In contrast with this type of deviant, there is the person who is very different from most people but whose deviant characteristic is neither immediately visible nor already known to the group he is currently in. The homosexual, the atheist, the communist, the light Negro, the pervert, the genius, and the criminal are all to some extent and in some circumstances non-visible deviants. These deviants can sometimes hope to conceal their differentness and to prevent the public or some segment of it from knowing that they are deviants. Since concealment, if it is successful, is probably the best defense against ill treatment, it would be expected that these nonvisible, unknown deviants should try to conceal their differentness when they can.

There is some anecdotal and observational evidence that deviants do try to conceal their differentness. Goffman (1963) has written at length about the tactics of concealment. He describes how Negroes pass as white, stutterers avoid difficult words, blind people sometimes sit in dark rooms so that people do not notice their blindness, and so on. Based on his observations Goffman states: "Because of the great rewards in being considered normal, almost all persons who are in a position to pass will do so on some occasion by intent (p. 74)."

A very effective means of avoiding discovery by a particular group of individuals is to avoid contact. For example, Goffman cites the case of a homosexual who does not want his parents to find out about his deviation and tries to minimize the amount of time he spends with them. The more interpersonal contact there is, presumably the more likely it is that the deviancy will be discovered. This kind of avoidance of contact may be a somewhat extreme instance, but the minimization of contact or more important of close intimate contact must be quite common. It should occur primarily or exclusively with unknown, hidden, nonvisible deviants; once the deviancy is known, concealment is, of course, impossible and other means of protection must be sought.

This technique of concealment by avoiding social contact may take a variety of forms. In a threatening situation or with a threatening group, the individual can in the extreme case try to avoid contact with another person or with the group entirely. Since this is often not possible and since it in itself might attract attention to him, he can minimize contact by talking little, spending time alone, choosing a single room in college, working alone, etc. Or, he can spend the usual amount of time with the other person or persons, but can be careful not to stand out in the group by not taking important jobs, not saying anything special, not taking prominent positions of either a spatial or social kind, and so on. This would minimize the amount of attention people would pay to him and would minimize the likelihood that whatever he is hiding will be discovered. All of these techniques will be used, when possible, more by unknown deviants than by known deviants, although the latter may to some extent also minimize contact in order to reduce the likelihood that they will be mistreated.

Known and Unknown Deviancy and Concealment

An experiment was designed in which concealment by minimizing contact was an alternative open to the subjects. Subjects were made to feel either deviant or nondeviant. Half of the deviants thought that the rest of the group knew they were deviant (known); half thought they did not know (unknown). All Ss were told that they were going to be members of a group working on some interesting problems and were given a choice of doing their particular task in privacy or while sitting around a table with the rest of the group. They were also asked to perform a task which would indicate how well suited they were to the work which their group would be doing, and their performance on which would be known to the group. And finally, they were asked to perform another task which would benefit the group but which was not scored in any way.

The basic prediction was that the unknown deviants would choose to work alone more than would any of the other groups and that the known deviants would not differ from the non-deviants in this respect. It was felt that the known deviants could not benefit from working alone, since they would be having some contact with the rest of the group in any case. In fact, choosing to work alone might antagonize the rest of the group and aggravate the situation. The unknown deviant, on the other hand, might be able to conceal his deviancy by mini-mizing contact, and in particular minimizing the relatively important crucial contact involved in the work itself.

A second possibility was that the unknown deviants would also work less hard on the public task in an effort not to stand out. This is based on the same reasoning as the major prediction —the notion being that the unknown deviants want to avoid calling attention to themselves and will, therefore, avoid having a particularly good (or bad) score. Since they were told what the average score was, they should tend to be closer to it than should the nondeviants.

We felt that the known deviants might actually work harder on the public task than the nondeviants. The reasoning behind this expectation was considerably looser and more speculative. Since the known deviants cannot hide their differentness and are concerned about being rejected by the group, one line of action would be for them to attempt to compensate for their deviancy in some way. A possible way of doing this would be to show that they were very good group members and should, therefore, be accepted despite their deviancy. To this end, they could work very hard on the public task, thus demonstrating how valuable they were to the group. That is, of course, quite speculative and does not follow directly from our previous reasoning. It was a possible outcome for which we were looking because it was assumed that the known deviants would try to do something as a result of being deviant.

Finally, although the secret task was included primarily as a control on the public one, it was also a way in which the deviants could demonstrate their willingness to work for the good of the group. No specific predictions were made except that we did not expect the same pattern as in the public task. The unknown deviants would have no reason to work less hard here since there was no danger of them standing out.

METHOD

Subjects were 77 freshmen males at Stanford University. An additional six subjects were dropped because they did not participate in both sessions of the experiment. Ss were paid $3.00. The first session was run in groups ranging in size from 6 to 30. It consisted only of taking the standard personality inventory. Several weeks later all subjects were contacted by phone and appointments for the second session were arranged. Subjects were run individually in this second session. When the subject arrived, he was told that the main point of the study was to investigate how groups work on problems and that we were setting up five member groups which we wanted to study over a period of time. The subject was told that he had been put in such a group and was handed a piece of computer print-out containing his name and four other names. The other names were fictitious, thus assuring that no subject knew any of the people in his group.

At this point the usual deviancy manipulation was carried out. The subject was given feedback on his performance on the personality inventory as well as the scores obtained by the other group members. For all subjects the rest of the group had obtained nondeviant scores on all scales. Half of the subjects had deviant scores themselves; and half had nondeviant scores.

Known vs. Unknown

One of the critical parts of the experiment was to make certain that some deviants thought that the rest of the group knew they were deviant, while other deviants thought the group did not know. This was accomplished by making it seem that their scores either were or were not anonymous. The sheet containing the names of the group members also contained the subject's code number (e.g., 54). With this number he could identify which of the scores on the personality test were his. For half of the subjects (known condition), the code numbers of all group members were supplied on the sheet. Thus, the subject could easily tell what scores each group member had gotten; and much more important, it was clear that all of the group members could tell which scores the subject had gotten. To reinforce this point, just in case it was lost on some of the subjects, the experimenter said: "Next to each person's name you will see the person's code number. We thought it might be useful for people to know where they stand relative to the other people in the group and when we have the whole group together we will explain more fully what this means so that everyone will know quite well where everyone else falls on each of the distributions." In other words, it was made extremely clear that the others would know where he stood.

For the other half of the subjects (unknown condition) no code numbers were supplied for the rest of the group, only the subject's own number was supplied. The subject and the other subjects could tell what scores the group as a whole had obtained since five scores were circled on the feedback sheets, but no one could tell which scores belonged to which person. This was reinforced by the experimenter who said in part: "You will notice that we have not told you which name corresponds with which number . . . the code numbers have been randomly assigned to people. Thus there is no way in which you can tell which number corresponds to which person." After giving the subject sufficient time to look over the "results" of the personality tests, the subject was given a short vague description of what we were having the groups do: "A concept formation and problem solving task in which each person works on his own part of the problem, but the group must work together to a certain extent or they will never finish the problem."

Public Task

The first thing that the subject had to do was to write random numbers. The rationale for this went as follows:

> The task that your particular group will be doing involves the ability to reject previously learned sets or ways of looking at things. In the past, we have found that it is extremely useful for a group to know how good people are at this so that the different parts of the task can be assigned most efficiently. Recently a test has been developed that is very good at predicting how good people are at this sort of thing. This test involves the writing of random numbers. Now it may seem to you that this is a pretty simple thing to do, but you will be surprised how hard it is to do. Obviously, anyone can write

random numbers for a short time—the test is to see how long you can write them and how many you can write. The results of this will be presented to the group at the first meeting for the assigning of the different parts of the task. Most people work 5 or 10 minutes at this and so far no one has worked over 15, so just tell me when you feel that you are through.

In front of and slightly to the left of the subject was a clock. When the *S* was ready to begin, *E* wrote on top of the graph paper that *S* was using, "Begin," and the exact time at which *S* was starting to write. In this way it was made clear to the *S* that he was being timed. *E* then said, "Just tell me when you feel that you are through," and sat down at a desk about 15 feet behind the subject. If the *S* had not finished after 20 minutes, *E* said, "As I said before, just tell me when you feel that you are through." Most *S*s took this as a cue to stop, as all but a very few stopped within three minutes after this statement.

Private Task

When the subject had finished the random numbers task, he was told the following:

Now we would like you to prepare some materials for the group that you will be in. It happens that the task that you will be working on requires a large number of triangles that are different from one another but all have the same perimeter. Each member of your group has worked, or will work, at this for a while so that we will get as many as possible. I think that you can probably see why we don't do this ourselves—as, if one or two people work at it, they all tend to be pretty much the same. Actually, the task is constructed so that the more the group has of these triangles, the easier it is for them to complete the task and also the more different kinds they have to work with, the easier it will be for everyone. All you have to do is to make triangles with a perimeter equal to the length of this wire. Try to make no two alike. As I have said, the more there are of these, the easier it is for everyone in the group. Generally, if everyone works about five minutes at it, it is sufficient, but if you feel like working longer, your group will gain by it. After you've made each triangle, just put it in this box with the others that people in your group have made, and that way they won't get mixed up with those of any other group or with the scraps.

55

The subject was then given about 150 3 × 5 cards, scissors, a straight-edge, and a piece of wire eight inches long. He also was given a box about 8 × 12 × 4 inches with a slot on top. In the box there were some cards and when E was putting it down in front of the subject he mentioned to the subject that it seemed that someone else in his group had already been in. In this way it was made quite clear to the subject that his work would be mixed in with the rest of his group. There was also no emphasis made about time as there was in the random numbers task.

Working Alone or Together

As E collected the scraps of paper from in front of the subject, he told S:

> Now it happens that we are setting up two different types of groups that differ from one another in one major respect. In one set of groups you will be working on your own part of the task in a separate cubicle and at the end of the session your work will be given directly to the experimenter. In the other groups you will be sitting around a table discussing the task as you work. In both types of groups each person will be personally responsible for his own part of the task. They differ, therefore, only as to whether you would rather work alone or with the rest of the group. Now you know the problem of scheduling as well as we do, so I think that you can probably understand why we can't guarantee each person his choice. So what we are doing is trying to find out how strongly you feel about whichever choice you make, and in that way we should be able to assign people most equitably. Could you tell me which of these choices best describes the way you feel?

The subject was then given a card with the following six choices typed on it:

1. Very much want to work with the group
2. Moderately prefer to work with the group
3. Slightly prefer to work with the group
4. Slightly prefer to work alone
5. Moderately prefer to work alone
6. Very much want to work alone

After this rating, a few additional questions were asked, the whole study was explained in detail, and the experiment was terminated.

RESULTS

Our major hypothesis was that unknown deviants would choose to work alone more than would either known deviants or nondeviants. Subjects indicated their preference on a six point scale ranging from 1 (much rather work together) to 6 (much rather work alone). The results are presented in Table 4.1 which shows the mean score for each of the four experimental groups. The overall effect of deviancy is not significant ($F < 1.0$) but both the effect of public knowledge and the interaction of knowledge and deviancy are (F's $= 4.34$ and 4.23, respectively). It is clear that the main finding is that the unknown deviants do prefer to work alone more than do any of the other groups. The difference between the unknown and known deviants is significant ($t = 2.81$, df 36, $p < .01$) as is the difference between the unknown deviants and the nondeviants ($t = 2.16$, df 57, $p < .05$). Given a choice of having their work open to public view or keeping it relatively private, these subjects who feel deviant but think that others do not know of this deviancy tend to prefer working alone.

TABLE 4.1
PREFERENCE[a] FOR WORKING ALONE

Subjects	Known	Unknown
Deviant	1.67 (18)[b]	2.85 (20)
Nondeviant	2.15 (20)	2.16 (19)

[a]Six = maximum preference for working alone.
[b]Figure in parentheses is number in the group.

There is also a slight tendency for the known deviants to show a greater preference for working together than do the nondeviants ($t = 1.48$, df 55, $p < .20$). This is, of course, not significant and should be considered suggestive at best. It does, however, fit in somewhat with our discussion of the known deviant's position. He cannot hide, and might, therefore, attempt to compensate for his deviancy by convincing the group that he is very valuable and should be accepted despite his differentness. To do this he might want his work to be public knowledge because otherwise he would not have a chance of showing off how good it was. Thus, he might want to work with the group in order to show off. The slight indication that known deviants do have a strong preference for working together is at least consistent with this line of reasoning.

Similar hypotheses were made in connection with performance on the public task. The unknown deviants would not wish to call attention to themselves and would do relatively little work; whereas the known deviants would use this as a way of compensating and would do relatively more work than the nondeviants. Amount of work on the task, which was writing random numbers on sheets of graph paper, may be measured in two ways: length of time spent working and quantity of work accomplished. The pattern of both of these measures is very similar, and for simplicity they have been combined by the use of standard scores into a measure of total work. These data are presented in Table 4.2.

TABLE 4.2
AMOUNT OF WORK ON PUBLIC TASK

Subjects	Known	Unknown
Deviant	4.53	3.70
Nondeviant	4.34	4.03

Once again the pattern is as predicted. The unknown deviants work the least and the known deviants the most. The scores are, however, extremely variable and none of the differences is significant. Thus, although there is some slight tendency for the results to be in the direction predicted, they do not provide much support for our original hypotheses. The only encouraging note is that the data from the private task (triangle production) do not show this same pattern. When the work is entirely private, there is actually a slight tendency for the unknown deviants to work harder than the known deviants. Once again this difference is not significant, but it may be taken as a very weak suggestion that our argument is on the right track.

The study does support our major notion which was that unknown deviants attempt to conceal themselves by avoiding or minimizing social contact; but it lends only minimal support to the further idea that they should also try to be inconspicuous by not working too hard on a public task. It offers suggestive support to the idea that known deviants compensate for their deviancy by seeking the limelight, maximizing contact, and working particularly hard.

These results provide additional evidence that is consistent with our assumption that deviants are concerned about the treatment they will receive at the hands of nondeviants. The difference between the known and unknown deviants in their preference for working together fits in very nicely with this idea and is somewhat difficult to explain in any other terms. Social comparison, at least, would not tend to produce this difference. Therefore, this finding is most consistent with an explanation based on the notion that deviancy arouses concerns about being rejected and that these concerns affect the deviant's behavior.

Summary: Deviancy and Affiliation

Our first expectation about the effect of deviancy on affiliation was that deviants would be especially careful in their choice of associates in order to minimize the likelihood of receiving mistreatment. Deviants should, to a greater extent than nondeviants, attempt to choose people who were likely to be accepting of them. We further reasoned that this should make deviants prefer affiliating with deviants to nondeviants and that this might hold even when the other deviants were different from the deviants who were making the choice. In Chapter 3 we saw in two studies that deviants did prefer similar deviants to nondeviants, but the preference for different deviants which we found in our first experiment did not replicate.

The second notion was that deviants would, when possible, try to conceal their deviancy. The idea was that this would be a very effective way of eliminating the danger of being deviant. If no one knows you are different, presumably they will not be able to hold your differentness against you. This led to the hypothesis that unknown deviants (i.e., those who were not known to be deviant by the rest of the group or at least who thought the group did not know) would try to avoid discovery by minimizing social contact and by being careful not to stand out from the group; whereas individuals who were known to be deviants would not use these modes of protection. The study described in this chapter strongly supported the expectation that unknown deviants would minimize social contact and lent some support to the notion that they would also avoid being conspicuous. In both cases the known deviants not only did not reveal these behaviors but also showed a stronger tendency in the opposite direction than did the nondeviants.

Thus our expectations have been generally borne out by the experimental evidence. The deviancy manipulation does have important effects on the subject's pattern of affiliation, and these effects are in the direction we expected. These findings are, of course, very encouraging. We are, however, left with the critical question of whether or not they are really produced by feelings of deviancy. That is, does our manipulation do what we have said it does—does it influence how deviant the subject feels? Although it is almost always impossible to give an unequivocal answer to this kind of question, it would certainly be comforting to have some additional evidence with which to consider it. In the next chapter we shall present some such evidence and shall attempt to evaluate the deviancy manipulation in more detail.

5

IS IT DEVIANCY?

Introduction

We have seen that the procedure which we have called a manipulation of deviancy produces several interesting and meaningful effects. It does do something to the subjects which has a significant effect on their behavior. We have discussed these effects in terms of feelings of deviancy which were presumably aroused by the manipulation. In these terms the results are at least reasonable and plausible — feelings of deviancy might be expected to produce the effects we have found. Before investigating other possible effects of this procedure, however, it would be highly desirable to be somewhat more certain that the manipulation was really doing what we have been saying it does. First, does it actually make the subjects feel deviant and second, is it this particular feeling that is causing the subjects in the experimental condition to act differently from those in the control groups? Although it is virtually impossible to provide an unequivocal answer to these questions, we can attempt to increase confidence in our interpretation of the results.

In the first place we may ask whether or not the manipulation, at least on the surface, appears to deal with deviancy? Is it plausible that it could make someone feel deviant? The answer to this seems quite clearly to be in the affirmative. The subjects are given an impressive series of tests; they are then given feedback on these tests which shows their scores compared to the normal range of scores and more specifically to the scores obtained by the small group they are in. These scores are nonevaluative and are never labeled in any way which could indicate some particular meaning. The "deviant" subject discovers that almost all of his scores are at the extreme of the distribution — at one end of some scales, at the other end of other scales, but always at the ends. In contrast, the rest of the group has more or less average scores on most of the scales. Thus, the deviant subject is decidedly different on these dimensions. Regardless of their meaning, he is being told that he is deviant in some unspecified way. It may be argued that this manipulation has other effects in addition to making the subject feel deviant but, at least on the face of it, we feel it looks like a manipulation of deviancy.

The second approach to our original question is to see if we can get some indication that the manipulation really did make the subject feel deviant. To this end, we included in our experiments a variety of checks on the manipulation. These checks and the findings are described in Chapter 2. The basic method was the straightforward one of asking the subjects to rate how deviant they thought they were. Some questions simply asked the subject to check where he fell on a scale ranging from "same" to "different." Another question asked him, "How different do you feel from most people of your age and sex?" A third asked: "Do you feel different from most of the people around you?" followed by "How different?" These checks are obviously quite weak: some came before the complete deviancy manipulation had been given and others came after a long and often complex series of procedures which followed the manipulation. Despite these weaknesses, all of the checks in each of the various experiments produced a difference in the expected direction between deviant and nondeviant experimental subjects. In all cases the deviants rated themselves more deviant than did the nondeviants.

In other words, the manipulation seems to have gotten its message across. When we wanted to make a person deviant, the rating scale indicated that he was more deviant than when we wanted to make someone nondeviant. There was naturally some overlap, but in general the manipulation was quite strong. These results indicate that, at the least, the subjects knew what they were supposed to believe; at the best, they really felt more deviant after going through the deviancy manipulation.

Unfortunately, this is a crucial difference and one that is extremely difficult to pin down. We may argue that the experimental findings themselves lend some support to our interpretation of the manipulation. These findings make good sense in terms of deviancy, and in general are what we expected differential feelings of deviancy to produce. There remains, however, the possibility that the manipulation is affecting something else besides deviancy and that it is this other factor which is producing our results. Although it is extremely difficult to eliminate this possibility entirely, there is some evidence available to support our position.

Internal Analysis of Affiliation Results

If the subject's feeling of deviancy is producing the results, those subjects who feel most deviant should show the greatest effect. That is, if we classify subjects on the basis of the manipulation check into high and low deviants, we should get the same pattern of results as we did from the experimental groups. Since this check presumably measures some combination of the experimental manipulation and some preexisting feelings of deviancy, it is most desirable to look at the data within each experimental group. Experimental deviants are divided into high and low true (i.e., self-rated) deviants; experimental non-deviants are also divided in that way. Then we may look at the affiliative preferences expressed by each of these groups.

TABLE 5.1

SELF-RATINGS OF DEVIANCY AND PREFERENCE FOR
AFFILIATING ,WITH DEVIANTS

	Experimental	
Self-rating	Deviant	Nondeviant
Deviant	8.33 (12)[a]	4.70 (10)
Nondeviant	6.25 (12)	3.08 (13)

[a]Figure in parentheses is number in the group.

This analysis was done for the first experiment based on choice of affiliates and is presented in Table 5.1. It may be seen that the groups order themselves very nicely. The high true deviants among the experimental deviants choose the most deviants to affiliate with; the low true deviants in the experi-mental deviant groups are next; the high deviant, experimental nondeviants next; and the low nondeviants are last. The two high deviant groups on self-ratings choose significantly more deviants than do the two self-rated low deviants ($F = 4.85$, $p < .05$). Thus, these results exactly parallel the results of the experimental groups. What we have called the deviant groups (i.e., experimentally produced) look very much the same as groups set up on the basis of the subjects' own ratings of their feelings of deviancy. This is even true among subjects who went through the nondeviant manipulation. Since they never experi-enced the deviancy manipulation, whatever else it was pro-ducing would not have affected them. Thus, the fact that even within the nondeviants the deviancy check predicts quite well to affiliative preferences is particularly encouraging. Any alternative explanation of the effect cannot argue simply that it was affecting something other than deviancy. It must argue that the questions designed to check on deviancy were also measuring this other factor. Although this is still possible, it becomes more difficult and the explanation in terms of deviancy becomes more likely and parsimonious.

The same kind of analysis was done for the experiment on concealment, but it is somewhat more complicated because the major point of the study involves differences between known and unknown deviants. We had four experimental groups: known and unknown deviants and known and unknown nondeviants. Since we are interested in the preferences of subjects who really think they are deviant (as opposed to comparisons within experimental conditions), we divided all subjects into high and low deviants on the basis of the questionnaire. Only those who rated themselves on the deviant side of the midpoint are considered deviants. This yields eight groups of somewhat unequal size. The means are shown in Table 5.2.

TABLE 5.2
SELF-RATINGS OF DEVIANCY AND PREFERENCE[a] FOR
WORKING ALONE

	Experimental			
	Deviant		Nondeviant	
Self-rating	Known	Unknown	Known	Unknown
Deviant	1.86 (14)[b]	3.63 (11)	2.40 (10)	3.00 (6)
Nondeviant	1.00 (4)	1.89 (9)	1.90 (10)	1.77 (13)

[a] 6 = maximum preference for working alone.
[b] Figure in parentheses is number in the group.

Our interest is primarily in the unknown deviants since these are the ones we expect to prefer working alone. There are actually three groups that might be considered unknown deviants. The subjects who were in the unknown deviant condition and also rated themselves deviant are most clearly unknown deviants. Since they have everything going for them in terms of being both deviant and unknown, we would expect them to show the strongest preference for working alone. They do. Other subjects who are deviant and unknown are those in the two non-deviant conditions who consider themselves deviant. The attitude scales that we distributed show them as nondeviants but they think they are deviant. Thus, all experimental nondeviants who consider themselves deviant are, in fact, unknown deviants and should prefer working alone. This is what we find. These two groups are the ones who show the next most preference for being alone. All other subjects are either nondeviants or known deviants; and we would expect them to show less preference for working alone than do the unknown deviants. They all do, and, with minor fluctuations, they do not differ among themselves. Taken together these three unknown deviant groups are significantly different from the other groups ($t = 4.57, p < .001$). Thus, the only three groups which should, according to our analysis and to our experimental findings, want to work alone are the ones having the strongest preferences in this direction.

For both experiments, analyses based on the subjects' own self-ratings are consistent with the experimental findings. It makes it appear that whatever the deviancy question is measuring is the same variable that is being manipulated by our experimental procedures. Since the questions are very direct queries as to how different or deviant the subject feels, there seems to be good reason for thinking that at least in part that is what his response indicates. Thus, in the absence of any evidence to the

67

contrary, we shall assume that the manipulation and the questions are dealing with feelings of deviancy and that it is these feelings that are producing our experimental results.

We now come to what is probably the most difficult question. Even if we may assume that we are manipulating something resembling feelings of deviancy, may we generalize from the particular kind of feelings we are producing to other feelings of deviancy that exist in the world? To put it another way, are we dealing only with some peculiar esoteric feelings which can be called deviancy but which are different from all other feelings of deviancy, or do our results pertain to feelings that actually exist outside of the experimental laboratory?

Unmanipulated Deviancy and Affiliation

One way of answering this question is to see whether people who consider themselves to be deviants behave in the same way as do the subjects whom we cause to feel deviant by our manipulation. The internal analyses we have just reported are based on self-ratings of deviancy made by our subjects and might be thought to bear on this question. However, these self-ratings are determined to some extent by the effect of our manipulation and only in part by the subjects' usual feelings about themselves. The results of these internal analyses thus cannot be interpreted entirely in terms of predispositional feelings of deviancy. What we need is a self-rating of deviancy uncontaminated by any experimental manipulation of that variable. If subjects who rate themselves as deviant without going through our manipulation show the same pattern of preferences as do experimentally manipulated "deviants," it would indeed be very encouraging. This is what we attempted to demonstrate in our next study.

METHOD

The method was identical in all respects to the replication described previously in Chapter 3 with one crucial difference; subjects did not receive any feedback on their performance on the personality tests. That is, they took the tests but were never told how they had done on them. They went through everything that the other subjects had but were not *made* to feel either deviant or nondeviant. One other small change was that early in the personality inventory a question was included to assess how deviant the subject felt. It was imbedded in a series of other questions and was worded as follows: "How similar or different do you feel from most other people of your age and sex?" This was answered on a scale ranging from extremely different to extremely similar. We could have done the study leaving out the personality inventory entirely, but we felt that it was important for the subjects to be as similar as possible to those in the experimental conditions so that the results could be easily compared. If the subjects in this study had not taken the inventory and the results had been different from those of the experimental groups, it could have been argued that the studies were not really comparable. Therefore, we attempted to make everything as similar as possible.

After the personality inventory, all subjects were told that we were thinking of setting up groups and were interested in the kinds of people they might want to be with. They were then handed a sheet containing personality scores of almost a hundred "subjects." The sheets showed the scores of these subjects on each of five scales including a final scale which was labeled summary scale. Ten numbers were circled on each scale (the same ten on all) and subjects were asked to choose among these circled numbers. For all subjects eight of the circled numbers

69

were nondeviant (right near the median) on all scales while two were deviant (one at each end). The explanation of the choice, the test, the reason for setting up the groups, etc. were identical to that in the earlier experiment.

In other words, in all respects the study was a replication of the earlier one except that in the present one all subjects were treated identically. There was no experimental manipulation of deviancy. Instead of comparing experimentally induced deviants and nondeviants, we are interested in the relationship between the subjects' ratings of their own deviancy and their affiliative preferences.

RESULTS

There are a number of ways of describing this relationship. The simplest is to look at the correlation between self-rated deviancy and preference for deviants in the affiliation choice. This correlation is .48 ($n = 19$, $p < .05$). Thus, to a significant extent the more deviant the subject considers himself, the more likely he is to choose deviants to affiliate with.

We may also divide subjects into deviants and nondeviants and compare their affiliation scores. Wherever we draw the line between the two groups, we find that deviants choose more deviants than do nondeviants. For example, we may call every-one on the deviant side of the midpoint a deviant and everyone else a nondeviant. Defined in this way, the deviants show a strong and remarkably consistent preference for deviants. Weighting a deviant first choice 3, second choice 2, and third choice 1, we find that deviant subjects ($n = 8$) have a mean score of 3.75, while nondeviants ($n = 11$) have a mean of 1.73 ($t = 2.33$, $p < .05$). This may be a somewhat arbitrary definition of deviants and nondeviants, but wherever we draw the line the results are the same. (Considering only those above and below the midpoint, the means are 3.75 and 1.89; considering only those who are more than one point from neutral, the means are 4.0 and 1.57; etc.). Thus, subjects who consider themselves deviant and those who consider themselves nondeviant seem to differ in just the same way on this measure as do experimentally manipulated deviants and nondeviants.

Summary

All of these findings are reassuring. They indicate that our experiments are dealing with feelings of deviancy, that this is what we are manipulating, and finally and most important, that it is these feelings which are producing the differences among our conditions. They also suggest that the feelings produced by our manipulation are similar to typical feelings of deviancy that people experience. Despite the somewhat specialized way in which we are attempting to produce feelings of deviancy and the particular kind of deviancy the personality inventory is probably perceived as tapping, this manipulation produces feelings that are similar to those felt by people in the real world. We have not demonstrated this unequivocally, but the evidence certainly provides consistent, strong support for this interpretation.

With this behind us, let us now turn to new problems. The choice of whom to affiliate with is only one, albeit important aspect of the deviant's social life. Perhaps even more basic is the question of how deviants and nondeviants actually react to and treat one another, and this is what we shall consider in the remainder of the book.

6

AMOUNT OF AGGRESSION

Introduction

In previous chapters we discussed the deviants' desire to protect themselves and how this influences their affiliative choices. Our main findings are that deviants avoid close contact with nondeviants when they can; and that when they cannot avoid contact, they prefer to affiliate with other deviants rather than with nondeviants, even if the other deviants are different from themselves. One implication of these findings has to do with deviants' expectations about how others will treat them. Presumably everyone wants to be treated as well as possible; and it seems that deviants are particularly concerned about this. Therefore, these affiliative preferences are probably due at least in part to the assumptions deviants make about how others will treat them. The preferences suggest that deviants assume explicitly or otherwise that they will be treated worse by nondeviants than by other deviants and that this is true even for deviants who are different from them. Is this assumption correct? How do deviants and nondeviants actually treat each other?

Other things being equal, it seems likely that a nondeviant will be more aggressive and less helpful or kind to someone who is different from him than he will be to someone who is not different. Conversely, deviants should treat other deviants better than they treat nondeviants. We would argue further, and this is really the critical point, that these tendencies would hold regardless of the dimension along which the differentness occurs. In other words, a deviant will receive worse treatment at the hands of someone who is not deviant than at the hands of any other deviant. These expectations are based on the affiliative patterns we have found, on anecdotal and survey evidence, and from the results of a few experimental studies in the literature. Let us look at this evidence briefly.

There is widespread belief that those who are treated worst by society tend to be deviants. This belief is presumably based on personal observations and evidence from sociological surveys of patterns of employment, housing, schooling, etc. There is little doubt that in the United States various minority groups are discriminated against in a wide variety of ways. Negroes, hippies, Jews, homosexuals, communists, and intellectuals have been targets of persecution and discrimination in recent American history. They have been denied jobs and housing, refused admission to clubs, treated unfairly by courts of law and by law enforcement agencies, and in general have been given less good treatment than the rest of society. We find little discrimination against white Anglo-Saxon Protestants as a group. Instead, these groups who are different from the majority of society are the ones who receive this mistreatment.

The fact that particular deviant groups in society are mistreated is not, however, a sufficient answer to our original question. We have suggested that deviancy per se leads to mistreatment, that simply being different, regardless of the dimension or direction of differentness, causes those who do not share this differentness to treat you badly. In other words, non deviants tend to treat all deviants less well than they treat other nondeviants. Is there any evidence to support this proposition?

In the first place it is clear that the particular dimension on which the person is different increases or decreases the intensity and frequency of the mistreatment. A given society or subculture seems to pick certain types of deviants, certain types of differentness to subject to particularly bad treatment. The Negro has certainly been thus selected in the United States. In addition the innate or assumed value of some deviant attribute will affect how much its owner suffers on account of it. The seven foot, 280 pound giant will probably suffer less than the three foot, 76 pound midget. The former will be physically assaulted less often, and he may even find himself the hero of a school or community because his height is a decided asset on the basketball court. The homosexual's deviant attribute, in addition to being different, is generally considered bad or evil by much of society. He will therefore tend to suffer more than will the shoe fetichist whose sexual enjoyment depends upon his partner wearing bright red boots. The fetichist is statistically more deviant since there are fewer who share his particular appetites; but because people probably consider his odd attribute less evil than they do the homosexual, the fetichist will be treated less badly.

In other words, as everyone knows, some deviations from average or "normal" are less acceptable than others. Also, patterns of discrimination and prejudice have developed more around certain deviant attributes than around others. The important question for our purposes is whether cutting across the particular dimension of deviancy and across particular prejudices there is a general tendency to mistreat anyone who is different.

It is difficult to answer this question with the evidence that is currently available. On the anecdotal level there are incidents and patterns of behavior which suggest an affirmative answer. In American high schools there has recently been concern about styles of hair and clothing worn by the students. Worried educators around the country have been disturbed by boys wearing long hair. Just why this caused such disturbance is somewhat difficult to determine. They argued that long hair is messy and dirty, but this argument loses considerable force because many of these boys had their hair beautifully waved or fixed in some other fancy style. In any case, the educators could have required neat and clean hair, regardless of length rather than objecting to long hair per se. At the same time girls began wearing very short skirts, and this too was found objectionable. Here the objection was that this was obscene, indecent, and generally distracting. On the face of it, this was perhaps a reasonable argument. The curious sequel is that teachers were also disturbed when the girls began wearing "granny dresses" which instead of being three inches above the knee were three inches above the floor. They could hardly be described as provocative or distracting. Although a number of complex explanations of these various reactions by teachers are possible, a very simple one is that they are objecting to anything which is very different from the usual pattern. This kind of anecdote does not in any way constitute evidence for this notion; but it does suggest, at least to the authors, that it may be correct.

Relatively solid evidence along these lines is also available. For example, Festinger, Schachter, and Back (1950) investigated interactions within a housing community. One of their findings was that people who deviated from the group standards received fewer sociometric choices than did nondeviants. The dimension along which the deviancy occurred did not seem to be critical although of course the study dealt with a limited number of dimensions.

Unfortunately, evidence of this kind which supposedly describes what actually goes on in society is impossible to interpret in any definitive way. There appears to be good reason to believe that many deviant groups are mistreated; it is certainly true that some groups are. The problem is that we have no way of telling whether the mistreatment is because the people are deviant or because of their particular deviant characteristics. Even in the anecdote about skirt length there may be particular prejudices about very long or very short skirts rather than some more general prejudice against differentness in dress. Thus, observing society may enable us to be quite certain that there is more discrimination against certain deviants than against most non-deviants, but it does not enable us to answer our original question as to whether or not deviancy per se leads to mistreatment by nondeviants.

Although there are no experiments which provide evidence on this exact question, there is a sizable psychological literature that is relevant. Many psychologists have been concerned with why certain people are singled out for mistreatment. Several theories have been proposed to explain this phenomenon, and a number of experiments have been conducted to test these theories. The dominant theory has for a long time been the so-called "scapegoat" theory of prejudice, and this is also the theory that has the most to say about our specific problem.

The major tenets of the scapegoat theory (Allport, 1944, etc.) are that when people are frustrated they tend to become aggressive and that when they cannot aggress against the actual cause of their frustration, either because it is unknown, immune, inviolate, or some other reason, they tend to look for someone or something else to blame for the frustration and to aggress against. That is, the person looks for a scapegoat on whom to take out his frustrations.

The theory also proposes that certain attributes tend to make someone a good scapegoat. The ideal scapegoat is as similar as possible to the real cause of the frustration, is easily identifiable, is different from the frustrated person, and cannot retaliate.

It is clear that accepting this list of attributes of the scapegoat would lead to the expectation that deviants would be well qualified to be scapegoats. Deviants are certainly different and they are often very identifiable—two of the critical attributes. No statement of the theory has explicitly said that all deviants, regardless of their particular characteristic, will tend to be objects of aggression; but the general statement of the theory is consistent with this stronger hypothesis.

There is a considerable experimental literature on scapegoating, which has been summarized by Berkowitz (1962) and Buss (1961). Unfortunately for our purposes this research is directed primarily at the proposition that frustration leads to aggression rather than at the question of who is chosen as a scapegoat. The research attempts to discover if expressed aggression actually increases when the person is frustrated; it is not investigating the characteristics of the person who is aggressed against. The standard paradigm is to frustrate someone, see how much aggression he expresses against various minority groups, and to compare this with his responses when he has not been frustrated. Usually the measure of aggression is simply statements of prejudice with the targets not being present, and is thus a very distant and somewhat doubtful type of aggression. In addition, it almost always uses as targets minority groups against whom there are well established prejudices, so that a momentary increase in aggressive feelings would be unlikely to produce a change in the subject's responses to the group. In any case, the critical question in all of this research is whether or not the frustrating procedures actually arouse aggressive impulses. Since we are primarily interested in what happens when such impulses are aroused, the findings of this research are of little help to us. Thus it appears that all we can glean from the ex-

77

tensive literature on scapegoat theory is some additional consensual support for the notion that deviants tend to be mistreated by nondeviants.

More recent formulations of this problem in terms of social learning theory (e.g., Bandura & Walters, 1963) do not take us any further than the original statement. The basic point of this new approach is that prejudice is learned, and more specifically, that we learn to aggress against people who are different from us. This position seems eminently reasonable. Surely prejudices are learned rather than innate (if that is the other alternative). The important question for a theory of prejudice or aggression, however, is why this is learned instead of learning to treat all people equally. In any case, for our purposes the main contribution is that these writers agree with the basic description of prejudice given in scapegoat theory. They seem to agree that there is such a thing as prejudice and that people who are different tend to be treated badly.

One contrary result is reported in a study by Kleck, Ono and Hastorf (1966). College students were faced with either a crippled or normal interviewer, and the critical measures were how long the subject talked and what he said. The results showed that subjects found great difficulty terminating the interview with the crippled person, and also tended to talk about topics and include content which would minimize the possibility of offending or hurting the cripple. This indicates that college students, at least, may be very sensitive about the feelings of certain kinds of deviants.

The study does not, however, reveal much about aggression toward deviants. In the first place, there is no real measure of aggression and no clear comparison of deviants and nondeviants. The main finding is that subjects are considerate of the cripple. This does not demonstrate that they would be less aggressive toward him if the occasion arose. Moreover, the cripple is a very special kind of deviant. There is a strong cultural norm that handicapped people should be treated well, which makes it difficult to generalize this finding to other kinds of deviants. Thus, the result is interesting but is of somewhat limited relevance to our current problem.

Although there has been a lot written about prejudice and many experiments conducted, none of this literature provides any hard data relevant to our problem. Everyone seems to believe that people tend to aggress more against people who are different, but no one has actually subjected this idea to a rigorous test. The few studies that are closely related dealt with treatment of specific types of deviants rather than deviancy in general. This literature is thus encouraging in the sense that the descriptions are fairly consistent; but it does not provide any solid support for these descriptions.

There is one experiment that does provide evidence directly relevant to the question of how deviants are treated. In a well-known study, Schachter (1951) formed small discussion groups and included in each group three confederates. Two confederates took a position quite different from that held by the rest of the group. One of these confederates (the slider) gradually changed his position until it coincided with that held by the majority. The other (the deviate) maintained the deviant position. The third confederate took and maintained a position similar to the rest of the group. Elections were held at the end of the discussion, with all members nominating each other for three committees—executive, steering, and correspondence. The descriptions of these committees made it very clear that they varied in their desirability with executive being the most and correspondence being the least desirable. In addition, the subjects ranked all the other group members in order of how much they would like them to remain in the group. The data from these elections and rankings provide a measure of how much each member was accepted or rejected, and also, in the case of the nominations, specifically how often he was assigned to a good job and how often to a bad job.

The first finding is that the deviate is rejected more than either a person who holds the majority opinion or the slider. When asked to rank members in terms of how much they would like them to remain in the group, most subjects rank the deviate very low. Given a choice, they do not want the deviate to be in the group. The slider, who ends up agreeing with the rest of the group, and the one who agrees to begin with are ranked about equally.

Second, the deviate is nominated for the worst job, the correspondence committee, significantly more often than would be expected by chance and is nominated for the best job, the executive committee, significantly less often than we would expect simply by chance. The nominations of the other members are at about the chance level for all committees. In other words, the deviate is rejected more and is given poorer jobs than members who do not deviate from the rest of the group.

One aspect of this study should be made clear. Deviancy is manipulated in a specific, unambiguous way. The deviate differs from the group in his opinions as to how to treat juvenile delinquency. He is different in this particular opinion. The result may thus be due to the particular nature of the deviancy rather than to the deviancy per se. Nevertheless, this study does provide some experimental verification of the idea that deviants will be treated less well by nondeviants than will other nondeviants.

With this background in mind let us return to the issue at hand. We have seen that deviants appear to act as if they believed that deviants would treat them better than would nondeviants and that both the anecdotal evidence and the various theories and studies in the psychological literature are consistent with this assumption. Therefore, it seems reasonable to begin our investigations with the hypothesis that deviants will be treated worse by nondeviants than by deviants. In addition, we would propose the stronger statement that this would hold even when the deviants are quite different from each other (e.g., at opposite ends of the same dimension). Despite all of the social support for this hypothesis (particularly the first part of it), it has not been subjected to a rigorous test. Two experiments were conducted to provide such a test.

Before describing the experiments let us make two distinctions which appear to be important in the present context. The first is between the arousal and the expression of aggression. This is particularly relevant when prejudice is involved because the conceptualization of prejudice tends to include both feelings and expression. For our purposes it is essential to note that simply seeing someone against whom you are prejudiced may not ordinarily arouse aggressive feelings. Only the most rabid anti-Semitic or anti-Negro person feels a twinge of aggression every time he sees a Jew or a Negro. If, however, he already is annoyed at something or has been frustrated and feels aggressive, he may be more likely to express this aggression against the object of his prejudice than against someone else. This is probably an obvious point, but it is sometimes overlooked.

The scapegoat literature suggests to us a second distinction: between selecting an object of aggression when you have a choice of several and expressing aggression against an already chosen object. By the time most people are adults, they have probably developed most of their prejudices against large groups of people and thus to a large extent they have already selected their favorite or preferred objects of aggression. Thus, most experimental or observational studies of aggression and prejudice involve not the selection of an object, but expression of aggression toward objects that have previously been classified according to desirability as victims.

On the other hand, there are many situations in which a person is faced with the problem of choosing an object of aggression from among people who have not yet been so classified. Most people do not have the opportunity to learn a complete set of prejudices and are thus, at least in this sense, neutral toward many significant groups in society.

Thus, there are two possibly distinct questions: Given a victim, how much aggression is expressed as a function of the victim's characteristics; given a choice of victim, who is chosen, again as a function of the characteristics of the possible victims and of the chooser.

Aggression Against Deviant and Nondeviant Victims

The first experiment dealt with the question of how much aggression would be expressed against a preselected victim. A boy has been convicted of stealing an apple (or maybe a Cadillac) and his sentence is in doubt; the student scored lowest on the exam and he will be given a D or an F; the third baseman has just let the ball trickle through his legs for the winning run and his teammates are waiting for him at the clubhouse; and so on. In each case we are concerned with how the obvious object of aggression will be treated. In particular our experiment deals with how the deviancy or nondeviancy of the object and the aggressor affects the amount of aggression that is expressed.

The experiment was designed so that deviants and nondeviants would have a chance to express aggression toward a deviant or a nondeviant who had already been selected. We wanted to do this in such a way that the aggression could be expressed anonymously, with neither the victim nor anyone else supposedly knowing when the subject was aggressing. It was felt that this would eliminate confusing and perhaps confounding effects of social pressure for or against hurting another person and of the possibility of retribution on the part of the victim. Finally, we wanted the subject to feel that he was really hurting the other person and that he was doing this more or less by choice, not merely on the orders of the experimenter. In this way we hoped to provide a realistic test of the notion that deviancy affects the amount of expressed aggression.

METHOD

The basic method was quite simple. Subjects were made to feel either deviant or nondeviant and were then given a chance to be aggressive toward someone who had just caused them to lose $5.00. This other person was either nondeviant or deviant, and if both subject and "victim" were deviants they were either similar or different from each other.

Despite this fairly simple design, the procedure was quite complex. The subjects were 105 girls from several high schools in the Palo Alto area. They were paid $2.50 for taking part in the experiment and were run in groups of four or five plus a confederate. When they arrived for the experiment they were given the usual personality inventory. Before they began, however, it was explained that the study had two parts and that for the second part one of the girls (whom we shall call the "learner") would be doing something different from the rest. She would be taking a free association test in which her task would be to give creative associations to a series of words. The experimenter then selected the person for this job by having each of the girls pick a letter from a box. It was arranged so that the confederate always had the "L" which made her the one for the job. This also clearly identified her and made it possible for all subjects to notice her scores on the personality test without knowing anyone else's. That is, they knew that her code letter was "L" but did not know anyone else's code letter except their own. Thus, they were presumably anonymous but still knew the "victim's" score.

After this selection procedure the experimenter further explained that there was one other thing the group would be doing. The National Science Foundation was doing a study on perception and had a complex apparatus available for doing it. They had asked the experimenter if he could get the cooperation of the girls in the study. It would take only a few minutes to take the perception test and NSF could pay each of them an additional $5.00 for doing this. A very impressive piece of equipment consisting of two large consoles virtually covered with buttons, lights, and dials was sitting in front of the room. This equipment actually did have a function at some time in its life and looked the part. With this explanation completed and all of the girls presumably anxious to earn the extra $5.00, the personality inventory was begun.

The feedback on the inventory was done as usual. The five experimental conditions were produced by appropriate results on the feedback sheets. For example, in the deviant subject, nondeviant victim condition, the subject received deviant scores and all others received nondeviant scores; while in the both-deviant condition, the subject and the victim had deviant scores, with the scores being at the same end of the scales some of the time (similar deviant condition) and at opposite ends the other half of the time (different deviant condition).

When all of the tests had been completed, the experimenter said that there were two additional tests for the learner. He handed her one of them and left the room. The learner finished the test and then, with E still out of the room, got up from her chair and wandered over to the "perception apparatus." After looking at it for a while, she played idly with a few dials and "accidentally" knocked over a small auxiliary piece of equipment that was sitting on top of one of the consoles. She quickly picked it up, replaced it, and returned to her seat. All of this was done rather casually.

The experimenter returned to the room shortly afterwards, gave the learner the last test, and collected her responses to the first test. He next collected the final test and left the room again. He returned in a few minutes with feedback sheets for all Ss. These sheets reinforced the previous picture that had been given of the learner. She had either extreme or average scores on both tests.

While Ss were looking over these last feedback sheets, the experimenter turned his attention to the perception apparatus. He flipped a few switches, turned a few dials and generally tried to give the impression that he was simply getting it ready for the test. After a while, however, he began to act more and more worried, feverishly manipulated various controls, checked the wiring, and so on. Finally he remarked that unfortunately the apparatus did not seem to be working at the moment. He said that it had been working just before, but for some reason was now inoperative. He then announced that this meant the subjects could not take the perception test and naturally could not earn the extra $5.00. He said that he was sorry and acted distressed by this turn of events. Although it was not stated explicitly, the obvious and seemingly inevitable implication of all of this was that the learner had broken the machine and thus cost the other subjects $5.00 apiece.

With this background, the free association test was begun. It was explained that during the test, the rest of the subjects were to act as judges. They were to rate each response as either creative or non-creative and indicate their decision by moving a switch which was in front of them and which was labeled "bad, shock" and "good, no shock." All decisions were supposedly anonymous. It was further explained that whenever a majority of the subjects judged the response to be bad, the learner would receive a "medium intensity electric shock." The rationale for giving shock was that it might "teach" her to give better responses. The learner was strapped into her chair, electrodes were attached, and a screen was placed so as to conceal her from the subjects. The wires from the switch boxes ran into a small console which ticked, whirred, and made other interesting noises and which supposedly administered the shock whenever the majority voted for it. In fact, of course, no shocks were ever given and the learner recorded from a hidden indicator how each of the subjects had voted. The test consisted of 30 stimulus words to which L gave a prearranged series of responses. The responses ranged from reasonably creative (e.g., book-worm) to clearly uncreative (e.g., sky-blue).

At the completion of the test, a short questionnaire was administered, and the experiment was explained in detail. The subjects were sworn to secrecy and thanked for their help.

Let us review the design of the study. Subjects are made to feel either deviant or nondeviant; one of their group (L) who is either a deviant or nondeviant breaks a machine thus costing them $5.00 each. The rest of the subjects are then given an opportunity to deliver electric shocks to L. It is assumed that the loss of the money causes them to be angry at L, that voting for shocks is a way of expressing aggression toward L, and that the deviancy or lack of it of S and L will be one determinant of how many shocks are delivered. Our hypotheses are: (1) Deviant L will be treated better by other deviants than by nondeviants; (2) this will hold even when the deviants are different from L; and (3) nondeviants will treat deviants worse than they will other nondeviants.

TABLE 6.1
NUMBER OF SHOCKS DELIVERED

Subjects	Similar deviant	Learner Different deviant	Nondeviant
Deviant	9.14[a]	12.91	13.38
Nondeviant		12.62	12.24

[a] All n's = 21.

RESULTS

The number of "shock" judgments made by the subjects in each of the experimental conditions is presented in Table 6.1. The deviant L is shocked least by similar deviants, next most by the different deviants, and most by the nondeviants. Although this pattern is consistent with our expectations, it is evident that only one group is appreciably different from the rest. The similar deviants deliver significantly fewer shocks than any of the other groups (t's range from 2.15 to 2.92 with all p's < .05). All other groups vote for essentially the same number of shocks. Thus, only one of our hypotheses is supported. Deviants are treated better by similar deviants than they are by nondeviants. The other two hypotheses are not supported: deviants are not treated significantly better by different deviants than by nondeviants, nor do nondeviants treat deviants worse than other nondeviants.

Before discussing these findings let us add one piece of information. In designing the experiment we were particularly concerned with obtaining a measure of actual aggression. We would like to be able to say that we were successful and that the difference between the similar deviants and the other groups indicates less aggression by the former. There is the possibility, however, that no aggression was involved at all. Perhaps the subjects were merely following orders and making judgments to the best of their ability, and the similar deviants were simply less critical than were the others. Although even this might be interesting, it would not, of course, tell us anything about aggression which is what we want to know.

The interpretation in terms of aggression says that L made the other subjects angry at her by breaking the machine, that this anger was expressed in their negative judgments of her responses, and that the difference between the similar deviants and the other groups indicates that the former is expressing less aggression. Assuming this is true, it would follow that if L did not break the machine, the other subjects would not be angry at her, their judgments would involve little or no aggression, and similar deviants should not differ from the rest of the groups in the number of "shock" judgments made. To test this line of reasoning, a follow-up study was done in which as much as possible the first study was duplicated except that L did not break the machine.

Subjects went through the identical procedure as that employed in the main study, but L did not get up and fool with the perception apparatus. As before, the experimenter could not make the machine work. However, when he discovered that it would not work he remarked merely that it was a delicate, unreliable machine and that it just wasn't working right at the moment. He apologized and said that unfortunately he could not pay the extra $5.00 since it was only for the special study. The rest of the study was run in the same way as the first one. It would seem that under these circumstances the subjects should feel little antagonism toward anyone, and certainly no particular antagonism toward the learner. If the fewer shocks voted for by the similar deviants in the first study were due to their avoiding expressing aggression, no such difference should appear in this study.

That is exactly what was found. With no antagonism aroused toward the learner, there were no differences among the five experimental conditions in the amount of "bad, shock" votes. In contrast to the previous results, the similar deviants voted for just as many shocks as did the other groups. The number of shocks voted ranged from 11.8 to 12.6 with none of the differences approaching significance (all t's < 1.0). The absolute level of shocks in this study is not strictly comparable to that of the main experiment, since the learner was much less visible in the second, the studies were run at different times and with somewhat different subject populations, etc. But the lack of difference between conditions in the follow-up does seem to support our interpretation that in the first study the judgments are at least partly expressions of aggression toward the learner and that the deviants avoid hurting the learner when she is deviant in the same way they are.

These studies, therefore, demonstrate one effect of deviancy on aggression. The finding that similar deviants aggress less seems to make good sense. At the simplest level it could be explained merely in terms of feelings of similarity or closeness to the victim. The deviant feels different from everyone around him and must feel especially close to the one other person who happens to be different in exactly the same way he is. If he does feel this way, it would be reasonable for him to be reluctant to deliver shocks to this person. The nondeviant, after all, does not feel isolated and different—he is similar to most of the people

89

around him. Thus, the fact that the nondeviant victim also happens to be like him should be of relatively little importance and should have little effect on amount of aggression expressed.

One interesting point is that different deviants are treated the same as nondeviants. It will be remembered that our first affiliation study found a preference for different deviants over nondeviants but that this failed to replicate. The current lack of difference between different deviants and nondeviants should perhaps be taken to indicate that the positive finding was not a real one. If different deviants are treated no better than nondeviants, there would be no logical reason to prefer the former's company. However, as we have noted before, these affiliative preferences are based on the subject's expectation, not necessarily on what actually happens. In addition, as we shall see in the next chapter, there is some evidence that deviants are somewhat nicer even to deviants who are different from them than they are to nondeviants.

Although the effect of similar deviancy is both strong and meaningful, the important and striking aspect of this study is not this one positive result—it is the negative result for the nondeviant subjects. There is a very slight trend in the expected direction, but we must conclude that there is no evidence to support the notion that nondeviants aggress more against deviants than against nondeviants. Despite the observational and anecdotal evidence, despite the fact that most people seem to believe it, and despite the strong intuitive appeal of the idea, the data do not support it. Nondeviants who were given a chance to hurt a selected victim did not seem to care whether the victim was a deviant or a nondeviant. In the next chapter we shall attempt to explain this and to provide evidence to support this common conception of the effect of deviancy on aggression.

7

AGGRESSION AND THE CHOICE OF VICTIM

Introduction

In the previous experiment subjects were given the opportunity to aggress against a selected victim. Under these circumstances nondeviants show little tendency to favor other nondeviants over deviants. It seems to us that the explanation of what seems at first glance to be a perplexing finding may lie in the notion of expressed aggression. There are really two quite distinct questions in the expression of aggression—how much and against whom. Once the victim has been chosen, the aggressor must decide how much to hurt him. Should he be sentenced to one or to five years? Should he be given a D or an F? How many shocks should he be given? Obviously there is a wide range of possible answers. Judges can be severe or lenient; teachers can be tough or easy graders; etc. The point is that the decision involves only how much the person should be punished, not who should be punished. Of course, it is possible that who the object is affects how much aggression is expressed, but at least in our study we found that this was true only for deviants with a similar deviant as victim. The lack of other effects in this one study is not convincing proof of their nonexistence. It does suggest, however, that if such effects exist they are not particularly strong under these circumstances.

This kind of situation, in which the victim has been selected and in which the amount of aggression must be determined, probably occurs fairly often in society. Another common situation is one in which hostile or friendly feelings are aroused and the person must choose someone toward whom to express them. These kinds of feelings are aroused by a wide variety of events from a good or bad meal, to getting a raise in pay or losing a job, to the weather, and so on. When something unpleasant happens and a man feels mean, hostile, or unfriendly, there is a tendency for him to express this feeling. He can walk around sneering at the world, kick a dog, punch a wall, play football, watch a boxing match, or instigate one. One of the most common ways of expressing aggressive impulses is to hurt someone. The question for us is whom the aroused person chooses for this undesirable position of whipping boy (scapegoat). It may be that whereas deviancy has relatively little effect on how much aggression is expressed against an already selected victim, it has a very substantial effect on the choice itself. This would explain the lack of finding in the previous study and reconcile it with the widespread belief that nondeviants aggress more against deviants than against other nondeviants.

If we look back at the scapegoat theory of prejudice, we may see that it also suggests that the choice of object is the crucial point at which mistreatment of minorities is determined. The theory asserts that when things go wrong for someone, when he is frustrated or hurt, he tends to pick on someone to blame for his troubles. Given this explanation of aggression against innocent bystanders, it would be quite reasonable that once a victim had been chosen (particularly if he were chosen by someone else), it would not matter particularly who the victim was. Other things being equal (e.g., no chance of retaliation by the victim), all the frustration the person felt would be expressed against this chosen object, more or less regardless of his particular characteristics. In direct contrast, the theory states that when a choice of object is to be made, the characteristics of the possible choices are very important. Specifically it is suggested that the ideal scapegoat should be unable to retaliate, be accessible, should have a history of being an object of aggression, and should be identifiable and different. The last attribute is obviously very relevant for our present discussion. Although deviants differ markedly in how easy they are to identify, they all have some characteristic that clearly sets them apart from nondeviants. Sometimes this characteristic is very visible as is the case with giants, dwarfs, Negroes (in a white society), the deformed, etc.; sometimes it is quite hidden as with many homosexuals, some deaf people, religious minorities, communists, and so on. But in all cases the attribute is there, and if known it makes the person very different from the rest of the group. Thus, the deviant, any deviant, makes a good candidate for scapegoat and should accordingly be chosen by nondeviants as objects of aggression more often than should other nondeviants.

Although there is little or nothing in the literature on this problem, it seems clear that when a deviant is choosing, the situation is quite different. If he is looking for an object on which to vent his rage, another deviant, particularly one who is similar to him, makes a very poor choice. The basic assumption of the theory is that scapegoating is a form of displacement of aggression. The scapegoat has not actually done the person any harm. The actual source of the harm, however, either cannot be identified or cannot be attacked; and the scapegoat takes its place. Under these circumstances a deviant would hardly like to place the blame on someone who was just like himself—this would be essentially blaming himself and would not serve the purpose of scapegoating which is to displace the aggression and also satisfy the person's hostile feelings. To aggress against a similar deviant would be like punishing himself. This may happen on occasion, but is an entirely different process and much less common probably than that described as scapegoating. Furthermore, for the deviant a nondeviant is in many ways an ideal scapegoat. The nondeviant is clearly different from the deviant, he may reasonably be blamed for this misfortune, he is identifiable, and so on. Thus, a deviant might be expected not only to avoid choosing similar deviants but also to prefer nondeviants as objects of blame and aggression.

The case of the different deviant is less clear. On the one hand, a deviant who is different from the chooser fits all of the characteristics of a scapegoat, particularly in that he is different and also identifiable. On the other hand, this person is another deviant and in that sense may be seen as similar to the chooser. The former consideration would tend to make a deviant choose the different deviant; the latter would make him avoid choosing him. Taken together they would probably counteract each other and cause the different deviants to fall between the two other groups. That is, deviants would choose different deviants more than they would similar deviants but less than nondeviants would choose deviants.

This discussion of choices of objects for aggression is meaningful primarily in contrast to expectations about choices that do not involve aggression. Saying, for example, that deviants will avoid choosing other deviants to receive electric shocks tells us nothing about aggression if it turns out that deviants also do this when the choice is for someone to receive a reward. In other words, in trying to describe the patterns of aggression shown by deviants and nondeviants we must contrast aggressive situations with nonaggressive ones. We must compare the choices made when the outcome is unpleasant with those made when the outcome is pleasant. With this in mind, we arrive finally at some hypotheses about how the deviants and non-deviants will choose.

Although we began this discussion with the scapegoat theory of prejudice, it must be admitted that our hypotheses are not in any true sense deductions from the theory. Rather, starting with the brief statements of the theory, we have attempted to present a rationale for our own notions about deviancy and aggression. Given this rationale, we are led to the following expectations: (1) Nondeviants will choose more deviants for punishment than they will for reward; (2) similar deviants will show the opposite preference, choosing more deviants for reward than for punishment; (3) different deviants will fall between in both situations. In addition, nondeviants will choose more deviants for the punishment and fewer for the reward than will similar deviants. This is really saying that deviants will tend to treat other similar deviants well, while nondeviants will treat them badly.

Selection for Pain and for Reward

METHOD

The method was similar to that used in the previous study with a few important changes. Subjects went through the deviancy manipulation and were made to feel either deviant or nondeviant. All subjects were made to believe that the rest of the group consisted of one deviant and three nondeviants. For deviant Ss the other deviant was either similar to or different from them. The subjects were told that for the second part of the study one of them would be taking a free association test.

This test was made to sound either extremely unpleasant or quite pleasant. It was either a good or a bad thing to be selected for this job. Then the subjects were asked to choose the person for this job by giving a rank to each of the other subjects. The dependent measure was simply who was chosen by each of the experimental groups.

The subjects were 66 high school senior girls from schools in the vicinity of Stanford, California. They were contacted by phone and offered $3.00 for taking part in a two hour study. They were run in groups of five. If, as occasionally happened, only four subjects showed up, a confederate was standing by and she sat in to bring the apparent group size to five. Each group consisted of at least one in each of the deviancy conditions, but was either a reward or punishment group.

In the punishment condition the task was described almost exactly as it was in the previous study. The girls were told that they would be judging the responses and that whenever a majority of them judged a response to be bad, the responder would automatically receive a moderately painful electric shock. In the reward condition no shock was mentioned. Instead the person chosen was going to receive an additional $2.50 for doing the extra work. The experimenter then explained that we did not care who did this job so we usually let the group decide for themselves. Then he asked the girls to list in order their choices for the job; they simply listed the four other girls by code letter in the order they wanted. This terminated the experiment.

To summarize the design: there are three groups of subjects, nondeviants, deviants with a similar deviant in the group, and deviants with a different deviant in the group. Half of the subjects are deciding who should be chosen for a painful task; half are choosing someone for a rewarding task.

RESULTS

Since there is only one deviant among the four other subjects, each person's choices may be described by the rank given the deviant. A rank of one means that the deviant was chosen first; four means that he was chosen last, etc. These data are presented in Table 7.1.

TABLE 7.1

MEAN RANK OF DEVIANTS IN CHOICE FOR
SHOCK AND REWARD

Subject	Choice[a]	
	Shock	Reward
Similar deviants	2.82[b]	1.27
Different deviants	2.09	1.73
Nondeviants	1.09	2.18

[a] 1 = deviant chosen first; 4 = chosen last.
[b] $n = 11$ in each cell.

Looking at the complete pattern of results it may be seen that there is a strong interaction between condition of the subjects and type of choice ($F = 7.63$; $df\ 2, 60$; $p < .01$). This interaction is due to the fact that the deviants pick deviants who are similar to them for a reward and avoid picking them for punishment ($t = 4.08$, $p < .01$); while nondeviants have the opposite preference — picking deviants for punishment and not for reward ($t = 2.52, p < .05$).

Within the punishment and reward conditions the results are also in line with our expectations. When the choice was for an unpleasant, painful job the nondeviants almost unanimously chose deviants; whereas the similar deviants avoid choosing the deviant. All but one nondeviant picked the deviant first when she was going to get electric shocks. The one other nondeviant chose the deviant second. In contrast, only two similar deviants chose the deviant first. Also as expected the different deviants fell between the two other groups. The differences between the nondeviants and each of the deviant groups are significant ($t = 4.75$, $p < .01$, and $t = 2.14$, $p < .05$, for similar and different deviants respectively).

An entirely different pattern prevails when it is good to be chosen. As hypothesized, the preferences are almost reversed. The similar deviants go out of their way to pick the deviant to get the extra money. They choose her either first or in three cases second. The nondeviants, on the other hand, are about evenly divided between picking her first or close to last. This difference between similar deviants and nondeviants is significant ($t = 2.04$, $p < .05$), but the different deviants fall in the middle, and this time are not significantly different from either group.

A possibly interesting result is that the different deviants show a marked bimodal pattern in both the reward and punishment situations. In both cases there is a very strong tendency for them to pick the deviant either first or last. Out of 22 choices the deviant is picked in first or last place all but once. This seems to fit with our previous discussions of the behavior of deviants toward other deviants who are different from them. We suggested that the deviants may perceive the different deviant in two quite different ways. Some may see the other deviant as very different from themselves because they are as far away on the relevant dimension as they can be; while others may see them as quite similar because despite their position on the particular dimension, they are also deviants and in that very important sense are like them. This would explain the bimodal pattern.

When the different deviant is seen as different, she is chosen for the punishment and is not chosen for the reward; when she is seen as similar, the choices are reversed. And in the former case, the preferences are even stronger than are the non-deviant's preferences because, of course, the different deviant is even further away from the deviant than she is from the nondeviant.*

If we look back once more at the affiliation situation, this result suggests to us that deviants may tend to prefer different deviants to nondeviants, but that this preference should not be as strong as for similar deviants. In a sense this is what we found. In both of the relevant affiliation studies different deviants were chosen more than nondeviants. In the first study this was a strong, significant result; in the second it was very weak and did not approach significance. Taken together, however, and in the light of our present finding, these data could be interpreted as indicating a slight preference for different deviants over nondeviants.

Taken as a whole the present study clearly supports our analysis of the effect of deviancy on aggression. As we expected and as generally held notions about deviants and minority groups would also make us expect, nondeviants chose deviants for punishment and not for reward. Thus, as the subjects in our affiliation studies appeared to assume, nondeviants do treat deviants worse than they treat other nondeviants; and deviants (even different deviants) treat deviants better than do the non-deviants. A comparison of the present study and the previous

*This latter point fits with the commonly expressed idea that some minority groups are even harder on other minorities than are the nonminorities. If the other minority is seen as different and the commonality of their deviancy is not taken into account, the other minority becomes a perfect target for aggression. Not only is it clearly identifiable, it is as different as it could be.

99

one appears to demonstrate, however, that the difference in treatment occurs primarily in terms of who is chosen to be given good or bad treatment rather than in how much bad treatment is given to someone who is already chosen.

Sometime these choices may be quite deliberate, as was probably the case with Nazi persecution of the Jews, or when the aging millionaire decides to whom to leave his money. But most of the time this is not so. Few people sit down and deliberately decide to be aggressive or friendly toward someone or some group. The white Anglo-Saxon Protestant does not spend an evening deciding whom to blame for the three feet of snow blocking the driveway, nor whom he should smile upon because the sun has been smiling on him for the last few days. Nevertheless, when he leaves the house the next morning and has to tramp through the slush, he may well choose to be disagreeable to the Negro who works on his left in the assembly line; and when his walk to the bus is through bright sunlight and the smell of cherry blossoms rather than through slush, he may buy a beer for the white man who works on his right. Thus, deliberate or not, the choice does lead to worse treatment of deviants.

Summary

We have seen that deviancy is an important determinant of how someone is treated. The strongest effect is on choice of object. We found: (1) Nondeviants choose deviants for punishment and not for a reward; (2) deviants choose other deviants for reward and avoid choosing them for punishment. We also found that when given an opportunity to express aggression toward an already chosen victim nondeviants did not differentiate between deviants and nondeviants, but deviants did avoid hurting a deviant who was similar to them.

8

CONFORMITY

Introduction

Whether or not someone is deviant has a considerable influence on patterns of affiliation and aggression. Both of these behaviors involve in a sense only one person. The individual is deciding whom to associate with, how much to shock someone, which person to shock and so on. Although the decisions obviously will affect others, the individual makes the decision by himself. What he decides, however, seems to be due at least in part to his expectation of how his and the others' degree of deviancy will affect their interaction. Let us turn then to a consideration of just what these effects might be.

One type of social interaction which appears to be particularly relevant is the social influence situation. When one person is trying to influence another, personal characteristics of the two have almost always been found to be important determinants of the result. Status, prestige, expertise, self-esteem, and many other similar characteristics affect the success of an influence attempt. It seems likely that deviancy also plays a role in social influence.

The deviant appears to be faced with several problems in a social influence situation. In the first place, we have been assuming that he would probably rather not be a deviant. If he can do anything which will reestablish him as a nondeviant, or which would appreciably reduce his deviancy, there should be some tendency for him to take this course of action. This should occur when either his own feelings of deviancy or another's impressions of him are involved. Note, however, that the nondeviant also would rather not be a deviant. Although he may be less immediately concerned about this problem and this consideration will generally be less salient for him, he does have more to lose because for the moment he is relatively well-off. Thus, any action which would cause someone to appear deviant may be avoided even more by the nondeviant than by the deviant.

A second concern of the deviant centers around the likelihood of being rejected or otherwise mistreated because of his deviancy. We have seen evidence suggesting that this causes him to conceal his differentness when he can, and also to prefer the company of other deviants to that of nondeviants. It should also probably make him avoid being conspicuous, calling attention to his deviancy, or angering others, particularly anyone who might hold his deviancy against him. Of course, nondeviants also have most of these motivations but probably they are not as strong in most cases.

A third concern, which to some extent conflicts with the others, occurs when the deviant is stuck with his deviancy. If there is no realistic way to convince himself or others that he is not deviant, he should presumably try to make the best of it. This may cause him to act as if: (1) He does not care that he is deviant; (2) there is nothing wrong with being different; and perhaps (3) he is proud to be different. Any analysis in terms of cognitive dissonance or other consistency notions would lead us to expect this kind of response. I bought this car which rattles, but I love it dearly and am happy to own it; I predicted the end of the world and it did not come, but I believe it more strongly than ever and will try to convince everyone else I am right. Similarly, I may be deviant which causes other to scorn and mistreat me, but there is nothing wrong with deviancy and actually I am happy to be different.

There are probably other concerns also, but let us stop with these for the present. What kinds of effects should these have on the reactions of a deviant in social influence situations? Let us begin with a consideration of conformity which in some senses is the simplest influence situation.

For purposes of this discussion, let us define conformity in the somewhat limited sense of agreement with another person or persons even when the individual privately disagrees. Conformity consists of going along with the group despite the fact that you think they are wrong or you would prefer to take a different course of action. In the typical conformity situation the individual finds himself confronted with a group of people with whom he disagrees. They all say that the Republicans are the better party, that the civil rights movement is going too fast, that Ben Hur is a great movie, that line B is longer than line A; while he happens to be a liberal Democrat, a strong supporter of the civil rights movement, a man of taste as far as movies are concerned, and he sees line B as shorter than line A. The others express their feelings publicly. They do not argue or try to be convincing — they simply say what they believe. At some point our hero must also say what he thinks. He is under pressure not to disagree with the group and there is ample evidence (Asch, 1951, etc.) that many people will conform under these circumstances. They will express an opinion which agrees with the majority even though their own private opinion continues to disagree with it. There is no suggestion that their opinion has changed; the important aspect of the situation is the overt conformity itself.

It would seem that conformity would be especially likely to be affected by feelings of deviancy. We have defined deviancy as being different from a peer group and our manipulation explicitly informs the subject that he is different from the rest of the members of his group. Since his deviancy consists of this differentness, publicly admitting to being different on any additional dimension should be a very salient act. This disagreement would accentuate, confirm, and call attention to his deviancy, whereas agreeing with the majority would tend to minimize his deviancy. Since the deviant is presumably concerned about being mistreated because of his deviancy and since we have seen that he does take protective measures to minimize the possibility of this mistreatment, perhaps we should expect that the deviant will conform more than will the nondeviant.

On the other hand, we must consider how the subject feels toward the group. There is evidence that the more the individual cares for the group and wants to be a member of it, the more he will conform (Dittes & Kelley, 1956; Schachter *et al.*, 1951; etc.). Since the deviant is told that he is different from everyone else in the group, he may feel less drawn to the group and therefore feel less pressure to agree with it.

And there are undoubtedly a number of other factors which could cause the effect to be in one direction or the other. At the moment we know too little about deviancy to be able to come to any firm conclusions about its probable effects on conformity. Instead of relying on our intuition, let us see what previous research has discovered.

The anecdotal evidence on this is very difficult to assess. Some minority groups, under some circumstances, do tend to assimilate to a great extent. They try to be as similar as possible to the majority and often tend to lose whatever distinguishing characteristics they had. On the other hand, it is also true that other such groups do not assimilate. On the contrary, they emphasize their differentness, refuse to conform to the norms of the rest of society, and even exaggerate their differentness. Jews in Spain during the Inquisition would be an extreme case of the former process, while the Black Muslims in the United States at the moment would be at the other end of the continuum. Just why some groups take one road while others take the other is not at all clear. Obviously, the Jews had excellent reasons for assimilating because it was the only way to stay alive. Also, it should be noted that they at least had the possibility of "passing." Negroes, on the other hand, cannot in most instances pass—they are easily identified as Negroes and they can do little about this. It may be that when you cannot hope to blend with the majority, you tend not to conform; whereas, if you can, it is relatively likely that you will. Naturally, there are many other factors operating here such as what you have to give up in order to conform, the danger of not conforming, what is to be gained by conforming, etc. Thus, this anecdotal evidence is unfortunately of little help in our present discussion other than pointing up the likelihood that the effect of deviancy on conformity may not be a simple one.

There have been quite a few experimental studies of conformity involving what the authors call "deviancy" or "deviants." In these experiments deviancy typically is manipulated by giving the subject the impression that his opinion on some issue differs from that of the rest of the group. Although we would ordinarily not favor this procedure because of the importance of the content of the specific issue, this technique may make the subject feel somewhat deviant. The problem with these studies in terms of our present interest is that the conformity measures are then taken on the same issue which was used in the deviancy manipulation. That is, the subject is made to feel "deviant" and he is then given the opportunity to change his opinion so as to become less deviant from the rest of the group. This way of manipulating deviancy makes the study less useful for our purposes since we are primarily concerned with the effect of a feeling of deviancy on behavior which is not directly related to the cause of the deviancy. But an even more serious problem for our current concern with conformity is that these experiments provide no group with which to compare the deviants. A nondeviant in the experiment is defined as a subject who does not initially disagree with the majority. He is, thus, under no pressure to change his opinion and is accordingly not really in a conformity situation. The typical finding (e.g., Festinger *et al.,* 1952) that the deviant conforms (i.e., changes his opinion) more than does the nondeviant is relatively uninteresting since the former is under great pressure to change whereas the latter, who already agrees with the majority, is not. Thus, although this work is interesting from other points of view (e.g., communication patterns within the group), it unfortunately has little relevance to the problem of the effect of deviancy on conformity.

Another type of study which is more relevant involves placing a specific kind of deviant in a group which consists either of members of his group or of nondeviants. For example, Puerto Ricans and whites in New York City were faced with unanimous majorities composed of whites (Becker and Carroll, 1962). It was found that Peurto Ricans conformed more to the white group than did the whites. Unfortunately, this study and others like it confound the deviancy of the subject and of the group with a host of factors such as status differentials, expertise, etc. It is impossible to know whether the Puerto Ricans conformed more to the whites because of the former's deviancy, or because they wanted to be accepted by the whites, or because the whites had higher status, or what.

Another relevant study (Linde, 1964) used paraplegic and normal subjects and faced them with majorities consisting of paraplegics or normals. In this case, the paraplegics conformed more to the paraplegic majority and the normals conformed more to the normal majority. This study seems stronger than the previous one. As usual, the specific characteristic of the deviants and nondeviants is impossible to separate from the effect of deviancy per se, but at least the power and prestige of the majority is not confused with deviancy.

One point that should be remembered is that someone who is deviant on dimension X may gain very little by conforming on dimension Y. The fact that he is not different on Y does not make him any less different on X. It may, under some circumstances, make him more acceptable and it may at least draw less attention to him, but it may not make him appreciably less deviant.

It would seem, then, that whether or not deviants conform more than nondeviants may depend in large part upon the possible consequences facing them. If they are not going to have to interact with the group, if they anticipate no unpleasant consequences from not conforming or from being deviant (at least in this situation), there would seem to be little reason for them to conform more. In fact, it could be argued that they have good reason for conforming less. By maintaining their own opinions, they can say to the world and to themselves that they may be deviants, but they are willing to accept this. In addition, since they already think of themselves as deviants and presumably so do others, they have less to lose by not conforming. They are deviant on one dimension so it may not hurt very much to be deviant on another one (as long as this does not endanger them by calling special attention to them or by making them less acceptable to a group with which they must interact).

As you may see, we did not know what to expect regarding deviancy and conformity. It seemed likely that under some circumstances deviants would conform more than nondeviants, while under others this would be reversed. Just what the critical factors were, however, was entirely unclear. Therefore, we began this research keeping in mind the kinds of considerations described above but with no formal hypotheses or expectations.

Private Conformity to Normative Responses — Experiments I and II

METHOD

These two experiments were identical except for the subject populations employed. Experiment I used 45 high school girls while Experiment II used 64 college freshman men. The method was to give subjects the standard deviancy manipulation with half getting the deviant and half the nondeviant feedback. Then they were handed a questionnaire consisting of 25 true-false items selected from the MMPI. The items were chosen to be relatively innocuous (e.g., "I am very careful about my manner of dress." "It makes me angry to have people hurry me.") The subjects were told that the questionnaire was constructed so that they could compare their responses with those given by others. To this effect, it was explained that the answer given by "80% or more of a large sample of high school and college age girls (or college students for Experiment II)" was indicated on the sheet. The subject was supposed to read the item, look at the common answer, and indicate whether or not he agreed with this answer. The answers shown were randomly assigned to the items with 13 true and 12 false. The measure of conformity is simply how many answers the subjects agreed with.

RESULTS

In both studies the deviants disagreed with the majority opinion more often than did the nondeviants. The mean number of agreements in Experiment I was 14.48 for the deviants and 16.28 for the nondeviants; while in Experiment II the corresponding figures were 14.06 and 15.55. The differences between deviant and nondeviant groups are both significant (t's = 2.17, df 43, $p < .05$ and 2.37, df 62, p < .05, respectively). In other words, subjects who were made to feel deviant were less likely to agree with a normative response than were nondeviant subjects.

Other data provide additional verification of this result. In Chapter 5 we described a study in which subjects were run through our standard "personality test" but were not actually given any feedback on their performance. During the course of taking the personality test, however, subjects did rate themselves on how deviant they felt they were. This was done primarily to see how self-ratings of deviancy, without any confusion introduced by our manipulation, would correlate with the same kinds of behaviors we were investigating with the experimental manipulations. In addition to a measure of affiliative choice, the results of which we described previously, the subjects took the same conformity questionnaire used in Experiments I and II above. The results are exactly in line with those just reported. The correlation between self-ratings of deviancy and amount of conformity is $-.38$ ($p < .10$). In other words just as in our experimental studies the more deviant the person thinks he is, the less he conforms. This finding reinforces our confidence in the results of Experiments I and II and, incidentally, also provides more support for our assumption that our manipulation is affecting feelings of deviancy.

It should be pointed out that the procedure used in these studies is different from that traditionally used to study conformity. The subject is confronted only with a questionnaire on which the popular response is indicated. In the standard experiment he is confronted with a group of peers who are present in the room and who unanimously hold a position with which he privately disagrees. In addition, in the present study the subject's response is confidential, to be known only by him and the experimenter; whereas in the typical situation he must answer publicly. Exactly what effects these differences have or should have on the subject's behavior is unclear. But it does seem that it would be desirable to investigate the effect of deviancy on conformity in the more traditional situation. Therefore, let us postpone consideration of the present results until after we have described a series of experiments which employed the standard conformity procedures and we shall then turn to a discussion of all of the results involving conformity and deviancy.

Public Conformity to Unanimous Majorities

METHOD

Experiment III

The procedure was similar to that first employed by Deutsch and Gerard (1955) and its mechanical intricacies are described there. It involved the use of a so-called conformity apparatus to make each subject think that he was faced with a unanimous majority with which he disagreed. Subjects were 35 high school girls who were recruited through an ad in the newspaper. Upon arrival, the subjects were shown to the experimental room where they were seated in cubicles so that they could not see each other. The standard deviancy manipulation was then introduced, with subjects being assigned a code letter by drawing capsules out of a hat. Approximately half of each group was made to feel deviant, the other half made to feel nondeviant. Subjects were run in groups of five or six.

After the deviancy manipulation was finished, the conformity test was introduced as follows. "The next thing that we will be doing will involve a test of auditory perception. Your task will be straightforward. All you will have to do is listen to a series of clicks over these earphones (each subject had a set of earphones in front of her) and report the number that you hear. You will be reporting this number in two ways. In the first place, you will be writing it down on this sheet (the subject was then handed a score sheet) and you will also be pressing one of the three buttons in front of you to indicate the answer that you think is correct. On the score sheet, you will notice that there are three possible answers for each trial number. One of these, A, B, or C is correct for each trial. What you will be doing is to push the button corresponding to the correct answer when your turn comes up. You will also be writing down your answer, and everyone else's answer for each trial. In a minute I will give you a card telling you the order in which you will be answering. You can see everyone else's answer by watching the lights on the panel in front of you. For example, if it is Number 3's turn to answer and a B lights up, that means that Number 3 chose B for that trial. As you can see, the number of clicks corresponding to each letter for each trial (i.e., for the three different alternatives) is printed on the sheet in front of you."

The tape that the subjects listened to consisted of a series of clicks recorded from an electric metronome at the rate of 184 clicks per minute. At this rate it is quite easy to count accurately. The number of clicks in each series ranged from 14 to 40.

After a series there was a slight pause and then the subjects were called one by one (i.e., Person 1, Person 2, etc.). All subjects thought that they were Number 6 (or 5 in five man groups) and thus they all answered last. Before they answered, they had received feedback indicating how five (or four) other subjects had supposedly responded. On trials 1 to 10 the feedback indicated that everyone else had given the veridically correct answer. On 30 of the next 40 trials the rest of the group was shown to have given the incorrect answer. These 30 trials constituted the critical conformity trials. When the majority was supposed to be incorrect, the answer they "gave" was always one off from the correct one.

To sum up: the subject is in a room with five other subjects whom he cannot see. He hears a tape recording of some clicks and is supposed to indicate how many there were by pressing one of three buttons corresponding to three possible answers on the answer sheet. He responds last and watches the responses of the others on his panel. He records all responses, his own as well as the others. The feedback he receives on his panel is actually controlled by the experimenter. On 30 trials it appears that the rest of the group has unanimously chosen the wrong answer. The measure of conformity is simply the number of these critical trials on which the subject agrees with the incorrect answer given by the majority.

Experiment IV

This was identical to Experiment III with one change. The content of the items was personality questions rather than clicks. The experimenter read an item and the subjects were supposed to indicate their answer. It was thus comparable to the questionnaire studies except that the "normal" responses were indicated by false feedback from subjects actually in the room and the

112

subject's response was public. Subjects were 35 high school girls.

Experiment V

The procedure was identical to Experiment III except that instead of a conformity apparatus the subject actually faced three confederates posing as subjects, all responses were given verbally, and there were only 20 critical trials. Subjects were 30 freshman males at Stanford University.

RESULTS AND DISCUSSION

The amount of conformity shown by deviant and nondeviant groups in all experiments is shown in Table 8.1. It should be immediately apparent that there was no appreciable difference between the two groups in Experiments III, IV, or V. The means for deviant and nondeviant subjects are 12.27 and 12.35 for Experiment III, 16.33 and 14.41 for Experiment IV, and 6.47 and 5.93 for Experiment V. None of these differences even approaches significance nor are the differences in a consistent direction.

TABLE 8.1
NUMBER OF CONFORMING RESPONSES BY
DEVIANTS AND NONDEVIANTS IN FIVE EXPERIMENTS

	Experiment				
	I	II	III	IV	V
Subjects	Questionnaire personality items	Questionnaire personality items	Mechanical clicks	Mechanical personality items	Face-to-face clicks
Deviant	14.48	14.06	12.27	16.33	6.47
Nondeviant	16.28	15.55	12.35	14.41	5.93
t	2.17	2.37	<1.0	1.37	<1.0

In addition, if instead of the experimental groups we look at the subjects' own ratings, the data are no more encouraging. There was no consistent relationship between subjects' ratings of their own deviancy and their conformity scores.

Looking at the whole table it is clear that the specific procedure and content of the study make a big difference. Two experiments involved a questionnaire with the subject under pressure only to conform to a "general" norm rather than a specific opinion expressed by a group of subjects who were actually present. The subjects' responses in these studies were confidential — they would be seen only by the experimenter. In both of these studies there was a strong and significant effect of deviancy. The deviants conformed to the norm less often than did the nondeviants. In three experiments the subject was faced either directly or by use of the conformity apparatus with a group of peers who were in the same room and who unanimously held an opinion discrepant from his. The subject's response, moreover, was public — the rest of the group would hear it. Under these circumstances there was no appreciable effect of deviancy on conformity. What can we say about these results?

To begin with, there is our one positive finding — deviants conform less in the questionnaire, nonpublic situation. One explanation is that the deviants have less to lose by disagreeing that do the nondeviants. The deviants have been told that they are different. Disagreeing simply confirms this diagnosis — it does not threaten a favorable position. The experimenter presumably expects the deviants to be different from most people and will not be surprised if they are. Also, since he has based his opinion on very extensive and supposedly highly reliable tests, he will hardly be likely to change this opinion just because the deviants go along with the typical response. From the point of view of the deviant himself, agreeing with the norm will be

meaningless unless it is an honest opinion. Obviously, it is difficult to fool himself into thinking he is nondeviant by choosing a
response he does not really favor. Therefore, he has no reason
to conform and probably tends to answer honestly.

In addition, the deviant may have begun thinking of himself
as a deviant and may tend to behave in a manner consistent with
this belief. A previous experiment (Bramel, 1962) has shown
that giving subjects a particular image of themselves will cause
them under some circumstances to behave consistently with this
image. In our study we have told these subjects that they are
deviant. If they accept this evaluation, they may begin to
respond in a deviant way in order to maintain it.

The nondeviants, on the other hand, have been told that they
are OK, that they are like most people. If they disagree with
the normative response, they risk losing this enviable position.
The experimenter will be surprised at how different they are
and may wonder if they are indeed somewhat deviant. The subject may also be upset if he finds himself disagreeing often and
may tend to go along with the usual response so as to reassure
himself that he is indeed nondeviant. Thus, the nondeviant has
more to lose in both his own and the experimenter's eyes, and
he can maintain his position by agreeing more with the norm.

A final possibility is that the manipulation may have changed
the deviant subject's comparison group. Once he believes that
he is really a deviant, he may no longer compare himself to
groups of nondeviants. When he is shown how "most other
people" respond, he is not influenced because he does not consider himself a member of that group. In contrast, the nondeviant has been told that he definitely is like most other people
and he therefore should be influenced by how these others
respond.

We must point out that although these various explanations

sound plausible, they are offered after seeing our results. It would have been easy to argue, for example, that the deviant has more to gain by conforming and should conform more, but, of course, that does not fit the data. The explanations are accordingly highly speculative and should be taken as such. We think they make sense, but offer them only as suggestions.

A less interesting interpretation of the result is that the deviants are merely telling us what we just told them. They have just received feedback indicating that they are deviant. We then ask them whether or not they agree with the majority on a variety of issues. They say to us that, as we already know, they are somewhat different from the majority (i.e., they tend to disagree with the majority). The nondeviants similarly tell us what we have just told them, that they are quite similar to the majority (i.e., they disagree less often). Perhaps we have simply given the deviants permission to disagree or even urged them to disagree. If this is true, the results are relatively uninteresting. The effect is not due to feelings of deviancy but to a particular relationship with the experimenter.

The other studies produced consistently negative findings. Deviancy appeared to have little effect on conformity in a variety of experimental situations with several different kinds of stimuli.

How may we explain these negative findings in light of the "obvious" relationship between deviancy and conformity? Perhaps the simplest explanation is in terms of two conflicting tendencies on the part of the deviants. On the one hand, they appear to be less influenced by majority opinion than are nondeviants. As we have seen, when there is no direct confrontation and their responses are private, the deviants do conform less. On the other hand, the deviants may be more reluctant than nondeviants to reveal publicly that they disagree with the majority. When there is direct confrontation and responses are public, these two tendencies would operate in opposite directions. The deviants would be influenced less, but would also tend to conceal those disagreements that exist. Taken together, these factors could cancel each other and cause the deviants to show the same amount of conformity as the nondeviants. Although there is no additional evidence to support this explanation, it does fit the data quite well. One implication of it is that increasing the importance of the interaction between the subject and the source of influence should increase the relative importance of the second factor and should accordingly cause deviants to give in more to influence than do nondeviants. We shall see a demonstration of this in Chapter 10.

Another possibility is that those deviants who care a great deal about being socially accepted, will conform more than nondeviants; while those who care little, will conform less. The reasoning behind this might be that the former are very threatened by the possibility of being rejected and will do anything they can to reduce the risk; whereas the latter are not threatened, they realize that there is already a good chance they will be rejected whatever they do, and so the easiest course of action is to accept this and behave independently. We did obtain measures of subjects' general tendency to choose socially desirable alternatives by giving them the Marlowe-Crowne Social Desirability Scale (Crowne & Marlowe, 1960). This may not be a perfect measure of this characteristic, but the findings did not encourage us to seek further. There was no interaction between SD and deviancy in their effect on conformity.

Summary

We have two quite distinct results: (1) When confronted with a questionnaire on which normative responses are indicated

and when their own responses are to be seen only by the experi-
enter, deviants conform significantly less than do nondeviants;
(2) when confronted with a group which unanimously disagrees
with their opinion and when their responses will be public,
deviants and nondeviants do not differ in the extent to which
they conform.

9

ATTITUDE CHANGE

Introduction

Although attitude change and conformity have much in common, they differ in certain important characteristics. In conformity situations the opinion expressed by the group is often clearly incorrect (e.g., they say there were 20 clicks when there were actually 21). The group does not try to convince the individual but merely expresses its position; and finally even if the individual publicly agrees with the group, it is assumed that his private opinion has not changed. In attitude change situations, on the other hand, the issues are usually highly controversial with no obviously correct position, there is a determined effort to change the individual's opinion by argumentation or other direct means, and the goal is to produce a real change in his private opinion. Since the phenomena differ considerably, the somewhat discouraging results relating to conformity do not necessarily imply that deviancy will also have little effect on attitude change.

In order to distinguish it from conformity we shall investigate attitude change only when the individual need not express his opinion publicly. The subject is exposed to a communication which argues a position discrepant from his; then he is asked to state his own position in a confidential questionnaire. Under these circumstances the considerations which might affect his response are somewhat different from those in the conformity situation. In the first place, the subject need not fear the re-action of the source of the discrepant message. This person will not know the subject's response and obviously cannot be affected by it. This means that the subject need be concerned primarily with his feelings about himself and perhaps the experimenter's feelings about him. In this respect the situation is similar to Experiments I and II in the conformity chapter.

Secondly, the issue under discussion is controversial and argu-able, and the subject is accordingly free really to change his opinion on it. In contrast, in the conformity paradigm, the others' position is clearly false and presumably it is virtually impossible for the subject to change his private opinion.

We have suggested previously that the deviant would rather be nondeviant and accordingly he would like to convince him-self that he is not deviant. The attitude change situation may af-fect his feelings of deviancy. Hearing a position discrepant from his would probably reinforce his feelings of deviancy — this is one more thing on which he is different from other people. On the other hand, if he changes his position and agrees, at least on this issue he is not different from the other person and this should serve to reduce his feelings of deviancy. According to this analysis, the deviant should tend to change his opinion in order to agree with the discrepant communication more than should the nondeviant, who is less concerned about feeling deviant.

Although this analysis seems plausible, it entirely ignores whether or not the source of the communication is a deviant. There are at least two considerations which would seem to make this factor quite important. In the first place, if he is concerned about proving to himself that he is not deviant, the deviant subject has little to gain by changing his position so as to agree with another deviant. This merely emphasizes his deviancy. In contrast, agreeing with a nondeviant may reduce the subject's feelings of deviancy. If we assume that a nondeviant subject is generally less concerned about deviancy than a deviant subject, this line of reasoning leads to the expectation that deviants should be influenced more by a nondeviant than by a deviant source while nondeviants should not make this distinction or it should be less strong.

On the other hand, we must also consider the prestige and credibility of deviant and nondeviant sources. Certainly a nondeviant, someone who is presumably similar to most of the people in society, is generally felt to be more reliable than a deviant and should be more influential. But this feeling may be less strong for deviant subjects. Since they are themselves deviant, they may be more accepting of other deviants than are nondeviants. As we have seen, deviant subjects do prefer the company of deviants to that of nondeviants; they may also trust deviants more. In addition, deviants may consider other deviants their reference or comparison group; while for nondeviants other nondeviants serve this function. Thus, from this point of view, it seems likely that nondeviants will be more influenced by nondeviants, while deviants will show the opposite trend, or at least show this preference less strongly.

It is obvious that these two rationales lead to opposite predictions, and that taken together they suggest that the deviancy of the source of the communication will not interact with the deviancy of the subject. We shall discuss another aspect of the source later. At the moment we are left with the knowledge that the situation is extremely complex and that we do not know enough to come to any reasonable conclusions. Since it was impossible to construct any hypotheses in which we had much confidence, we began our studies only with the expectation that deviancy should have some effect on attitude change.

Deviancy of the Subject and the Source

EXPERIMENT I

Let us begin by describing a study which was concerned with two questions: (1) Do deviants and nondeviants differ in their overall amount of attitude change, and (2) what effect does it have if the source of the message is deviant or nondeviant?

Method

The basic design was to produce feelings of deviancy or nondeviancy with the standard manipulation and then have the subject read essays on two different topics. One essay was supposedly written by a deviant, the other by a nondeviant. The critical measure was the extent to which the subjects said that they agreed with the others' opinions.

Procedure

Subjects were 48 freshman males at Stanford University. They took the personality test in groups of three to ten and about two months later returned for individual sessions. This second session was described as a preliminary meeting to prepare the subject for later ones at which he would be in a group working on various problems. The subject was given feedback on the personality test which showed his scores as well as those of two other members of his group. One third of the subjects received nondeviant scores, the others received deviant scores. For all subjects one of the other members was a deviant, one a nondeviant. When the subject was deviant, half of the time the the other deviant was described as similar to the subject (i.e., he received deviant scores at the same end of the scales as the subject), half of the time he was different. There were thus three groups: non-deviant subjects with a nondeviant and deviant in the group; deviant subjects with a nondeviant and a similar deviant; and deviant subjects with a nondeviant and a different deviant.

It was then explained that we wanted to acquaint the subject with the type of work his group would be doing, and also with the reactions of these other members of the group. He was given two business case histories to read. After he had read the first one, he was given a handwritten essay on it, supposedly composed by one of the other group members. He then indicated how much he agreed with the essay, how good the arguments were, how much he thought he would like the author of the essay, and a number of other questions. The subject next read a second case history, an essay on it by another group member, followed by the same rating scales.

The two case histories were similar to those used by Canon (1964) and Freedman (1965). Each described a decision that a business man had to make, with the various alternatives being about equally desirable. The essays supposedly written by the other members both favored the alternative that the previous studies found to be somewhat less popular. The two case histories, the source and handwriting of the essays were all counterbalanced.

After completing both cases and both questionnaires, the subject was given some additional questions, including how much he thought each of the other members would like him, how honest he was, and, as a check on the manipulation, how similar or different he thought he was to most people. The experimenter then explained the study to the subject, and asked him not to talk about it. This terminated the experiment.

Results

The results can, unfortunately, be summarized with the brief statement that no differences of any kind were found in amount of agreement. Although a check on the deviancy manipulation showed that it was successful, and despite differences found between the deviants and nondeviants on measures relevant to other problems, the agreement measure showed nothing. The three groups did not differ in how much they agreed with the opinions, nor in which opinion they agreed with more. There was approximately equal agreement with the opinion of the deviant and the nondeviant.

Some possibly interesting incidental results were found. Each subject rated both the deviant and the nondeviant on how good his arguments were, how good he would be in the group, how easy he would be to get along with, and how much he thought he would like him. Correlations between each of these ratings and the extent of agreement with his opinions revealed a consistent pattern. For all experimental groups and for both deviants and nondeviants the correlation between agreement and the first three ratings are high and positive. Subjects agreed more with the person whose arguments were better, who would be better in the group task, and who would be easier to get along with. There were no appreciable consistent differences among the three groups in the magnitude of these correlations. However, on the last scale, how much he would like the other, a big difference occurred. Whereas for both deviant groups the correlation between liking and agreement was high and positive (ranging from .29 to .54) for the nondeviants there was essentially no correlation between these two measures (−.19 for the deviant and .10 for the nondeviant). A similar result was found in the correlations between agreement and ratings of how much the other would like the subject. These were high positive for the deviants (.24 to .71) and essentially zero for the nondeviants (.03 and .08).

It is, of course, risky to make too much of a few correlations

chosen from a large group of intercorrelations, and our specula-
tions here should be taken as such. Since we cannot help speculating, however, this finding seems to suggest that the deviants
are more concerned about disagreeing than are the nondeviants,
but that a critical factor is their perception of how much they will
like and be liked by the other. When they agree, the deviants
perceive the other person as likable and as liking them; when
they disagree the opposite is true. This effect could work in
either direction. The deviants could be more inclined to agree
with people whom they like and whom they think will like them;
or conversely, they may think that agreeing with the person will
make him like them and that consequently they will also tend to
like him. In either case, and we cannot differentiate with our
data, the deviants make this connection between agreement and
liking while the nondeviants do not. This would seem to be one
more indication of the former's greater sensitivity to and concern about their relationships with other people in the group.

Although the results of this study were quite unencouraging,
we felt that perhaps it was not a very good test of the effect of
deviancy on attitude change. In several ways the design of the
experiment probably produced a rather weak situation. In the
first place, the manipulation of deviancy was not done in a
group. When this manipulation is done individually, it appears
to be less effective than when the subject can look around and
compare himself to four or five other people. In the individual
situation he is told that he is different from most people, but
these other people are not there and he must take it all on faith;
in the group situation, it is more convincing and powerful. Secondly, one of the people who wrote the essays was described as
deviant and one as nondeviant. This meant that for the deviant
subject, there were in essence two deviants and one nondeviant
in the group of three. He apparently accepted this, but it must

have greatly weakened the feeling of being different. After all, he was in the majority.

Finally, the communications were written and there were two of them. They were thus much less convincing than a direct, oral, single communication would have been. For all of these reasons, we decided to do another experiment to assess the effect of deviancy on attitude change in a somewhat stronger situation.

EXPERIMENT II

Method

Subjects were 46 Stanford freshman males who were paid $2.00 for the experiment. Two subjects who had heard about the study were omitted, leaving 11 in each condition. They were run in groups of five or six with one of the members of each group being a confederate. The standard deviancy manipulation was given. Some of the subjects were made to feel deviant, some nondeviant; and the confederate was described as either nondeviant or deviant. If both subject and confederate were deviant, their scores were similar (i.e., they were similar deviants). There were thus four conditions: both deviants; subject deviant, confederate nondeviant; subject nondeviant, confederate deviant; and both nondeviant. At least one person in each condition was included in each group session.

Procedure

After the subjects had taken the complete personality inventory, but before they had gotten the feedback on the last subtest or the summary feedback, the experimenter described the second part of the study. He said that we were going to ask one of them to give an extemporaneous talk on some subject, and that we were interested both in what kind of talk he gave and in the other subjects' reactions to the talk. He then picked a letter out of a box and indicated that "D" was to be the one to give the talk. "D" was, of course, always the confederate. The experimenter said, "Here's your topic" and handed "D" a piece of paper. He continued: "You should have about five minutes to prepare your talk while I score the last test." The rest of the subjects were not told at this time what the topic was.

In about five minutes E returned with the final feedback sheets, gave the subjects several minutes to look them over and to notice where "D" stood on them, and then asked "D" to begin his talk. In all cases the topic was: "Should graduate students do a greater percentage of undergraduate teaching than they now do, with professors doing correspondingly less?"

The confederate had carefully rehearsed his speech and, while it was not identical each time, it was very similar. Previous testing had indicated that practically all students at Stanford are strongly opposed to this proposal. The confederate began by saying that when he saw the topic his immediate reaction was quite negative, but that on thinking it over while trying to come up with arguments, he had decided that actually he was in favor of it. He then proceeded to give what we hoped would be a convincing argument in favor of the proposal. He delivered it in a somewhat halting, repetitive manner so as to make it seem not rehearsed and thereby to minimize any suspicion. He spoke for about five minutes. At the end of the talk E distributed questionnaires and asked the subjects to fill them out.

The questionnaires contained questions on agreement with the speaker, ratings of the quality of his arguments and of the talk as a whole, plus items relating to impressions of the speaker. When the questionnaire was completed, E explained the purpose of the study and terminated the experiment.

Results

Our major interest is in the amount of agreement with the speaker as a function of his and the subject's deviancy. These data are presented in Table 9.1. It is apparent that deviancy had little or no effect. The four groups agree with the speaker to virtually the identical degree. The differences between conditions are so small that there is not even any indication of a trend. None of the comparisons, main effects, or the interactions produces an F greater than 1.0. In other words, as in the previous study, deviancy does not seem to influence the reaction to a discrepant communication.

TABLE 9.1
AGREEMENT WITH SPEAKER'S POSITION[a]

	Speaker	
Subjects	Deviant	Nondeviant
Deviant	46.64	46.82
Nondeviant	50.36	45.82

[a] 0 = maximum agreement; 90 = maximum disagreement, $n = 11$ per cell. All F's < 1.0.

These two studies thus produced little evidence that deviancy is related to attitude change. On the contrary, they appear to indicate that overall susceptibility to attitude change is not affected by feelings of deviancy and also that the deviancy of the source is similarly unimportant. Despite these negative findings, our original idea that the source of the communication would interact with the deviancy of the subject continued to sound plausible. It seemed, however, that the critical variable might be whether or not the discrepant message came from a peer of the subject.

Since the subject's deviancy is defined in terms of a peer group, it should be his agreement or disagreement with the peer group that concerns him. Disagreeing with an authority figure or some irrelevant group signifies little or nothing about his main problem. Agreeing with the president of the university certainly does not imply that a student is not deviant. It may even imply the opposite, since these days, in particular, students tend to disagree more than they agree with authority figures. When the disagreement is with a peer group, however, it signifies a great deal. To the extent that the individual is defined in relation to this group, his agreement makes him non-deviant while disagreement makes him deviant. Thus, according to this rationale, deviants should be more concerned with agreeing with peers than with authorities.

If we can assume that nondeviants, at least in this non-threatening situation, are less concerned about being deviant, they should be relatively more influenced by the arguments themselves and the prestige of the source. Since authority figures generally carry more weight than peers, it might be thought that nondeviants would be more influenced by the former than by the latter. In any case, from this analysis we would expect that deviants would change more when the communication came from peers than from an authority, whereas this difference favoring peers would be less or even reversed for nondeviants.

We should note that in the previous studies the persuasive communications came from peers and the deviants and nondeviants did not differ in the amount of attitude change. However, the first experiment suffered from many defects including the weakness of the deviancy manipulation and the use of two different communications; both studies lacked measures of the subjects' initial position and were in addition confused by the source being either deviant or nondeviant. Therefore, it seemed desirable to conduct a study which eliminated some of these weaknesses and also explicitly varied whether the source of the communication was a peer or an authority figure.

Peer vs. Authority as Source of Influence

METHOD

The basic design was to make subjects feel either deviant or nondeviant, present them with a discrepant communication from either an authority or peer group, and measure the amount of attitude change.

PROCEDURE

Subjects were 47 freshmen men at Stanford University. They took the personality inventory at one session and returned in groups of three to six several weeks later. At this second session they were given feedback on their performance on the tests, with some receiving deviant and some receiving nondeviant scores.

After receiving this feedback, subjects went through two procedures designed to disguise the main point of the study, and then the attitude change manipulation was presented. Subjects were told that we were interested in how they judged another's personality from what he had written. Previously they had been asked to judge their own personality and those of the other subjects present, and this introduction was therefore probably quite plausible. They were then presented with a two page essay on the topic of whether or not professors should be relieved of teaching duties so that they could devote more time to their own research. The writer of the essay argued in favor of this proposal. All subjects had some weeks before been given a questionnaire in an introductory psychology course and they virtually all were strongly opposed to decreased faculty teaching. The position taken in the communication was thus very discrepant from that held by the subjects.

The communication was supposedly an abbreviation of a committee report. For half of the subjects (authority group) it was described as being "written by the chairman of a special committee appointed by the Association of American Colleges, an organization that includes virtually every institution of higher learning in the United States. The committee consisted of nine authorities in the field of education and included representatives from government and private foundations, large and small universities and colleges." The other half of the subjects (peer condition) were told that the report was "written by the chairman of a special committee appointed by the LASSU (the Stanford student legislature). The committee consisted of nine Stanford male students and included members of every class. The members were selected to be as representative as possible of the whole student body, and represented a wide variety of major fields, living groups, and other activities. The author is a Stanford junior." This description was designed to eliminate the possibility that the subject would decide it was not a representative group or that its members were different enough from him that he could ignore their position.

The communication was, of course, identical for all subjects. It began by saying that the committee's initial reaction had been negative but that it had reversed its position on the basis of various critical arguments which it then presented. This was done to make it plausible that a student group would back the proposal and also to make the faculty group appear reasonable and liberal so that it would be more persuasive.

CHAPTER 9

After reading the communication, subjects answered a number of questions about it. The key question asked the subject how much he agreed with the proposal that "professors be relieved of teaching obligations in order to devote more time to research." This was answered on an undivided scale labeled "disagree very much" at the left and "agree very much" at the right. The identical question had been included in the prequestionnaire so that change scores could be used.

RESULTS

As in our other studies, there was no overall effect of deviancy on attitude change. The deviants changed an average of 6.17; the nondeviants an average of 5.91. This very slight difference does not approach significance.

TABLE 9.2
ATTITUDE CHANGE AS A FUNCTION OF
SOURCE OF COMMUNICATION

Subjects	Source	
	Authority	Peer
Deviant	4.62 (13)[a]	8.00 (11)
Nondeviant	6.16 (12)	5.64 (11)

[a] Figure in parentheses is number in the group.

In contrast to these unpromising data are the figures on the interaction of source and deviancy. These results are presented in Table 9.2. It may be seen that who the discrepant communication comes from has an important effect on how deviants and nondeviants react. Nondeviants are slightly more influenced by an authority than they are by a peer, whereas deviants are considerably more influenced by a peer than by an authority. The difference between peer and authority conditions within the deviant group is statistically significant ($t = 2.11$, $p < .05$), and the overall interaction of deviancy and source is marginally significant ($F = 3.64$, $p < .07$).

Our interpretation of this result centers around the idea that deviancy is defined as being different from a peer group. If the deviant is concerned about minimizing his deviancy, he should be concerned primarily about his relationship to peers. Agreeing with a peer (even privately) tends to minimize his feelings of deviancy, while disagreeing with a peer increases these feelings. In contrast, agreeing with an authority is either irrelevant to these important feelings of deviancy or may increase feelings of deviancy if the authority is seen as holding views discrepant from most of the individual's peers. Therefore, to the extent that the individual is concerned primarily about his feelings of deviancy, he should be influenced more by a peer than by an authority.

The nondeviant is also concerned about not being deviant, but less than is the deviant because the former is relatively secure in the knowledge of his own lack of deviancy. The nondeviant should thus be less concerned about disagreeing with a peer. This does not imply that the nondeviant will necessarily be more influenced by the authority than by the peer (although that is what we found). The direction of this difference in any given situation will obviously depend upon many factors including the strength of the nondeviant's concern about being deviant, the prestige of the authority, the relevance of the issue, etc. The important point is that regardless of the particular situation, compared to each other, the deviant should be relatively more influenced by the peer while the nondeviant should be relatively more influenced by the authority.

Summary

What can we say about the effect of deviancy on attitude change? In the first place, there is little evidence from our three experiments that deviants differ from nondeviants in their overall tendency to change their attitudes when they are attacked. In none of the studies is there any appreciable difference between the two experimental groups, nor is there any consistency in the direction of the small differences. The results indicate that deviancy has either a weak or no overall effect on attitude change.

The results of the last study suggest a reason for this lack of effect. We found that deviants are more influenced by a peer than by an authority figure, whereas nondeviants show a weak trend in the opposite direction. This finding seems to reinforce our belief that the deviant is strongly concerned about minimizing his deviancy and that other things being equal he will act so as to produce this effect. When, as in an attitude change situation, he can reduce his feelings of deviancy by agreeing with a peer group he will do this. When he cannot do this, because as in the conformity situations the disagreement is too strong or too straightforward, he will generally be influenced less than a nondeviant.

10

COMPLIANCE

Introduction

A somewhat different type of social influence occurs when one person complies (or fails to comply) with a request made by another. In this situation there is no attempt to change someone's attitude nor to produce conformity with a group's response. Instead the goal is to induce the individual to agree to perform some action which he would ordinarily not perform. A typical instance is a charity appeal. The prospective donor is asked to give money to a cause which he is presumably in favor of, but which he might not support unless directly approached. Under these circumstances greater pressure on the individual in terms of rewards, threats, social pressure, etc., will increase compliance, as will a variety of other factors such as whether or not this is a first request, the individual's feelings of guilt, and so on. It seemed likely that deviancy would also affect compliance.

Research on compliance is relatively recent and limited and tends to concentrate on situational factors. None of this previous research involved deviancy directly. A number of studies have shown that making someone feel guilty increases his tendency to comply (Carlsmith & Gross, 1968; Freedman, Wallington, & Bless, 1967). Although this tells us nothing about deviancy, it does demonstrate that how the subject feels and in particular how he feels toward the person making the request is one determinant of how compliance occurs. Other than this very general notion, however, this work has little direct relevance to the problem of deviancy and compliance.

Our findings on conformity and attitude change are also not particularly illuminating. The most consistent results were that in a face-to-face situation deviancy had no overall affect on susceptibility to social influence, whereas in an anonymous situation deviants were influenced less than nondeviants. We did find that deviants were influenced more by peers than by authority whereas nondeviants showed the opposite trend, but the deviancy of the other person seemed to make no difference in terms of attitude change. Despite these somewhat negative results, we steadfastly maintained our confidence in the hypothesis that deviants should be more easily influenced than nondeviants. This was based primarily on the rationale that deviants are in a more sensitive, fragile position and that they would therefore find it more difficult to resist pressure and more advantageous to succumb.

The compliance situation is actually quite different from the subject's point of view from conformity or attitude change situations. When someone disagrees with you in the conformity or attitude change studies, he may not care very much whether or not you change your opinion. He thinks there are 21 clicks, you think there are 20; or you say that you dream frequently and he does not. Although he would probably like you more if you agreed with him, he should not be very upset by your disagreement. And of course if your responses are anonymous, you need not worry about his reactions at all.

The compliance situation is an entirely different story. Here someone is right across the table from you asking you to do something for him. He needs help and wants you to help him. Obviously he cares a great deal how you respond. If you agree, he will presumably be very grateful and appreciative; if you do not agree, he may or may not be angry, but you will certainly not endear yourself to him. From the standpoint of the deviant subject, it must be clear that agreeing to help will minimize the likelihood of bad treatment. In particular, if the other has any tendency to hold his deviancy against him, this tendency should be reduced. He would clearly treat the subject less badly if he had just agreed to do a favor for him. The same is true for the nondeviant subject, but since he is probably less concerned about being mistreated in this situation he should be less likely to comply.

A second reason for expecting more compliance by the deviant is that he is probably thinking somewhat badly of himself. He has found out that he is somewhat odd and he would rather not be. Doing the other person a favor does not reduce the subject's deviancy, but it may make him feel better because he is doing a "good deed" and thereby demonstrating what a nice guy he is. In other words, he may be deviant but he is really OK anyway. Once again, the nondeviant probably shares this motivation but less strongly.

The deviancy of the person making the request may also affect the degree of compliance. From the point of view of the deviant subject, there is more to gain or lose when confronted with a nondeviant than a deviant. Assuming that the subject is concerned about being mistreated by the other, he is obviously more likely to feel apprehensive when the other is a nondeviant than when he is deviant. After all, the nondeviant is presumably going to object more strongly to the subject's deviancy and mistreat him because of it. Thus, to the extent that concern about mistreatment tends to increase compliance, the deviant should be more concerned about mistreatment by the nondeviant than by the deviant and should accordingly comply more to the former than to the latter.

Nondeviant subjects, on the other hand, are supposedly less concerned about being mistreated. To the extent that they are worried, they might actually be more worried about the deviant than the nondeviant, since the deviant is different, odd, and perhaps antagonistic. In addition, the nondeviant may feel that it is more of a "good deed" to help out the deviant than just another average person. Therefore, it seemed that the nondeviant subject might comply more with the deviant than with the nondeviant.

To summarize, we started with two main expectations: (1) Deviants should comply more than nondeviants; (2) deviants should comply more to a nondeviant than to a deviant, whereas nondeviants should show this preference less or even have an opposite preference.

Agreeing to a Request Made by a Deviant or a Nondeviant

METHOD

The subjects were 60 freshmen men at Stanford University. They were generally run in groups of six, consisting of four real subjects and two confederates. When the subjects and confederates had all arrived, they were split into pairs—two pairs made up of one confederate and one subject each, and one pair of real subjects. If, as happened occasionally, only two or three real subjects were present, the extra pair was omitted or the odd subject run alone. (This all-subject pair played no part in this experiment—it was included primarily to make all subjects believe that six people were present.)

Each of the experimental pairs (i.e., one subject and one confederate) was put in a separate room. The two members of each pair sat at opposite ends of a table with an opaque divider between them so that they could not see each other. They were then given the standard deviancy manipulation. The feedback was in terms of six scores, corresponding to the six subjects in the session. The code letters of both members of the pair were indicated very clearly so that the subject knew the scores the other was receiving, and also knew that the other would be aware of his (the subject's) scores.

There were four experimental conditions: the subject was either a deviant or a nondeviant and the confederate was either a deviant or a nondeviant. When they were both deviants, their scores were similar. In order to make certain that the confederate would not systematically affect the results, he was kept blind to the subject's experimental condition. This was done by giving the confederate the same meaningless feedback sheets in all conditions and not allowing him to see the sheets the subject received.

Approximately two minutes after the last piece of feedback had been given out, and while the experimenter was out of the room, the confederate got up, walked around to the subject's side of the table, and made the crucial request as follows: "Excuse me. I was wondering if you'd be willing to do me a favor. I'm working for an organization that is trying to save the Redwoods and we've been sending out a standard letter to a lot of people to see if they're interested in helping us. Now, if they are, we send them more information, and we've found that a hand-written letter is fantastically effective — it has a personal touch to it that really works. So, would you be willing to take some names and addresses and send this letter to them?"

The confederate then waited for the subject to answer. If he was asked any questions he tried to answer them by paraphrasing the original request. If the subject refused to take any names, the confederate sat down. If the subject said he would take some names, the confederate continued: "We try to get people to take as many as fifty. How many do you think you could take?" The confederate waited for a number and then returned to his seat. This terminated the experiment.

RESULTS

The measure of compliance was the number of names the subject agreed to take. Due to the skewed distribution, a square root transformation was performed. Table 10.1 presents means based on these transformed scores. Our first expectation was that the deviants would comply more than would the nondeviants. This is what happened. The deviants took more than twice as many names as did the nondeviants (14.98 and 7.22, respectively). This difference is significant ($F = 5.49$, df 1,56, $p < .05$).

TABLE 10.1
COMPLIANCE TO DEVIANTS AND NONDEVIANTS

Subjects	Person making the request	
	Deviant	Nondeviant
Deviant	12.82[a]	17.14
Nondeviant	11.90	2.53

[a]$n = 15$ per cell.

Our other expectation was that the deviants would comply more to a nondeviant than to a deviant, while the nondeviants would show a smaller or opposite preference. The pattern of results is in this direction. The appropriate statistical test is the interaction between deviancy of subject and deviancy of requester which is significant ($F = 4.47$, df 1,56, $p < .05$). Thus, both expectations are borne out by the data. Deviants do comply more than nondeviants, and this effect is particularly strong when the request is made by a nondeviant.

It should be noted, however, that much of the difference among groups is contributed by the nondeviant-nondeviant cell. This group complies considerably less than any other (p's range from $< .10$ to $< .05$). This raised the possibility that compliance in this cell has been for some reason inhibited rather than the other cells being increased. Although we cannot be certain which is occurring, data from other studies suggest that the amount of compliance in the other three cells is high rather than that in the nondeviant-nondeviant cell being unusually low. In several experiments involving a request similar to that used in this study, control conditions produced compliance approximately equivalent to that found in our low cell (Carlsmith & Gross, 1968; Freedman & Schiffenbauer, 1967). These other control conditions are not, of course, identical to the nondeviant-non-deviant cell in the present study, but they do seem to be roughly comparable. In other words, it seems to us that a mean of 2.5 is not inordinately low and it therefore seems unlikely that compliance has been inhibited in this condition. It seems considerably more likely that this constitutes a reasonable baseline and that compliance has been raised in the other three conditions.

Assuming this, it is then somewhat surprising that the amount of compliance in the nondeviant subject-deviant requester condition is so much higher than when the nondeviant makes the request. Although the direction of this effect was expected, the magnitude was not. It is perhaps unnecessary to pay much attention to such a result. It may be due to chance, to the particular issue that was chosen, or any one of a number of similarly uninteresting factors. On the other hand, if we take the result at face value, it seems to demand more of an explanation than that offered in our previous discussion.

One possibility with broad implications is that nondeviants in general may under some circumstances be extremely sensitive to the demands of deviants. We usually think of the deviant as being less strong and more compliant, and this seems to be true much of the time. However, the deviant may sometimes have considerable power. Perhaps being different, being an unknown or less well-known type, has advantages. We suggested earlier that it might seem more dangerous to refuse a deviant than a nondeviant, because the former is less predictable. Or the strength may lie in being different per se and thereby being in some sense more of a person, more individual. This is, of course, sheer speculation. Whether or not there is such an effect and when it will and will not occur is for the moment unknown. This is one of the many questions which future research will have to settle.

Our major results are that deviants comply more than nondeviants, and that this difference is larger when the request is made by a nondeviant than when it is made by a deviant. Both of these findings were expected and they fit in nicely with our previous discussion. The deviant's fear of mistreatment should cause him to be more compliant in general, and should be particularly strong when the requester is a nondeviant.

The finding that deviants comply more than nondeviants contrasts with what we discovered about the effects of deviancy on conformity and attitude change. It will be remembered that in no study were deviants influenced significantly more than nondeviants; and that in several studies in which they did not have to interact with the source of the pressure, deviants actually conformed and changed their attitudes less than nondeviants.

This pattern of results is quite consistent with our previous suggestion that deviants are actually influenced less than nondeviants, but are more reluctant to disagree publicly. It seems likely that increasing the intimacy and importance of the personal interaction should increase any tendency the deviant may have to avoid open disagreement. Accordingly, the compliance study, which did have direct confrontation between the subject and the source of the influence, should have produced greater compliance by the deviants; whereas the conformity and attitude change situations, which involved relatively little or no direct interaction, should not. If this analysis is correct, the greater compliance by deviants should depend in large part on this direct confrontation between subject and requester, and it should disappear or be reduced when the confrontation is eliminated.

Compliance without Direct Confrontation

Method

To test this, a study was conducted which was similar to the previous one in most respects except that there was no direct confrontation between the requester and the subject. In the first study, the subject and confederate were alone in a room, the confederate faced the subject and made the request. In this second study, the subject was alone in the room or with one other subject. The experimenter entered the room, and said, "Could you please fill this out while you're waiting for the next part. It's something someone in the department asked me to hand out." He then handed the subject a sheet of paper on which the request was written and left the room. The request was identical to that used previously. The subject was supposed to indicate whether or not he would help and if he would, how many names he would take. If he agreed to help, he was supposed to give his name—otherwise he could leave it blank. In

143

all other respects the experiment was the same as the first one. Subjects were 30 freshmen men at Stanford University.

RESULTS

As before, a square root transformation was performed because of the skewed data. The means are presented in Table 10.2. It may be seen that with this less intimate, less direct request, the effect of deviancy is quite different. Deviant subjects take an average of .40 names, while nondeviants take 2.59. Although this difference is only marginally significant ($t = 1.71$, df 32, $p < .10$), it suggests that deviants are less compliant in this situation than are nondeviants. It certainly indicates that the previous finding, that deviants are more complaint, does not hold up.

TABLE 10.2

AMOUNT OF COMPLIANCE TO WRITTEN REQUEST

Deviant	Nondeviant
.40[a]	2.59

[a] $n = 17$ per cell.

The finding, therefore, reinforced our belief that only when there was direct confrontation would deviants comply more than nondeviants. The results of a final study lent even more support to this idea.

Compliance in a Mail Survey

METHOD

Two hundred names were chosen from the San Jose telephone directory and were then assigned at random to one of the two experimental conditions. All subjects were sent a Department of Psychology envelope containing a postcard on which the request was printed. Subjects were asked to answer two fairly innocuous questions: "Compared to most people, how much TV do you watch? Compared to most people, how much reading do you do?" They answered by circling the appropriate choice (much more, more, about the same, less, or much less) and could then simply drop the postcard in a mailbox since it was stamped and addressed.

The experimental manipulation consisted of how the subject's household was described in the introduction to the request. For half of the subjects the card read: "Dear Sir: You have been chosen to participate in this survey because in many ways your household is very similar to others in this area. We are interested in how this relates to the questions below. We would greatly appreciate your filling out and mailing this card as soon as possible." The other condition was identical except that in the first line the subject was told that he had been chosen because his household was "very different from others in this area." We intended this manipulation to mean that some subjects were told that they were deviant, while others were told that they were nondeviant.

RESULTS

Compliance is measured simply by whether or not the subject answered the questions and returned the card. Whereas 46.4% of the "similar" subjects returned it, only 29.6% of the "different" subjects did.* The difference is significant (chi square = 5.16, $p < .05$). In other words, telling people that they are different from most of the people around them makes them less

*Percentages are based on less than 100 because some envelopes were returned undelivered.

them makes them less likely to return a postcard than if you tell them that they are similar to most people.

Summary: Deviancy and Social Influence

When the situation involves little direct confrontation of the subject and the source of the pressure, deviants conform, change their attitudes and comply no more or sometimes less than nondeviants. When the subject is confronted directly by the person making the request, deviants comply more than non-deviants, and this difference is particularly strong when the request is being made by a nondeviant. In addition, although there is no overall difference between deviants and nondeviants in attitude change, deviants are more influenced by peers than authorities whereas nondeviants tend to show the opposite effect.

These findings, while not as strong as those on affiliation or aggression, are generally consistent with our previous discussions of the considerations which cause deviants to behave differently from nondeviants. The evidence continues to suggest that deviants are concerned about mistreatment. However, whereas the effects on affiliation and aggression were quite direct and reasonably simple, the effect on social influence is more complicated. The major implication of this work is that how deviancy affects behavior in a social influence situation depends greatly on the particular circumstances. We are inclined to interpret the findings in terms of two conflicting factors. The deviant has a general tendency to be less influenced than a nondeviant. However, the deviant is also concerned about being mistreated and is therefore reluctant to expose his differentness publicly. The more intimate and threatening the situation, the greater this reluctance becomes. These two tendencies conflict and produce different results in different situations. When there is little personal contact with the source of influence, or when for some other reason the situation is non-threatening, the deviant will appear less persuasible than the nondeviant. As personal contact and resulting threat increase, the deviant will give in to pressure more and more, and with direct confrontation and high threat, the deviant will succumb to influence more than the nondeviant.

11

SUMMARY

We have presented a series of experiments dealing with the effect of deviancy on various types of behavior. Let us briefly list our major findings.

Affiliation

1. When their deviancy is not publicly known, deviants will attempt to avoid close contact with others. When their deviancy is public knowledge, they will not do this.

2. Deviants prefer to associate with other deviants rather than with nondeviants. This may hold even when the other deviants are different from them.

One question concerns the extent to which this preference for deviants is due to social comparison processes. As we mentioned in Chapter 3, our manipulation of deviancy probably tended to arouse some uncertainty in deviant subjects regarding the nature of their deviant characteristics. This may have produced strong needs for social comparison which would, in turn, cause them to seek out people who were similar to them. It should be possible to separate the effect of this process from the effect of the feelings of deviancy per se. This might be done by producing deviancy without arousing so much uncertainty, by increasing the likelihood of rejection, or by decreasing the possibility of social comparison. We reported one study in which deviancy was not manipulated and subjects' self-ratings of deviancy correlated with their preference for other deviants. This suggests that these preferences are, at least to some extent, produced by deviancy rather than uncertainty. Nevertheless, it would be valuable to have an experiment specifically designed to investigate this problem.

Aggression

1. Given the opportunity to aggress against a previously chosen individual, deviants hurt a deviant who is similar to them less than they do a nondeviant or a different deviant. The most important result, however, is that all other groups are similar and in particular the nondeviant does not hurt the deviant more than he does the nondeviant. But,

2. when asked to choose someone to receive electric shock, there are big differences between deviants and nondeviants. The deviants select nondeviants more than deviants; whereas nondeviants have the opposite preference. In contrast, when the choice is for someone to receive a reward, all of this is reversed — with deviants picking other deviants and nondeviants picking other nondeviants.

We interpreted this result as supporting the common assumption that nondeviants tend to mistreat deviants. However, it indicates that the main effect is in the choice of object rather than in the amount of aggression that is expressed once the victim has been selected. This finding does suggest that the deviant's apparent concern about mistreatment at the hands of nondeviants is justified, but it seems to deny that the mere presence of a deviant will cause this mistreatment. Rather the sequence appears to be that once aggressive impulses are aroused (by something else), the deviant is likely to be the object upon which they are vented.

Social Influence

1. *Conformity.* In face-to-face situations, with responses public, there was no overall effect of deviancy. When normative responses are presented on a questionnaire and subjects respond privately, deviants conform less than do nondeviants.

2. *Attitude change.* There was no overall effect of deviancy. In addition, the deviancy, or lack of it, of the cource of the communication had no effect on its influence. The one clear finding was that deviants are influenced more by communications from peers than by an authority, whereas nondeviants had the opposite preference.

3. *Compliance.* With direct confrontation deviants complied more than did nondeviants, and the difference was largest when the person making the request was a nondeviant; with no direct confrontation, deviants complied less than nondeviants.

These results indicate that the effect of deviancy on social influence depends greatly on the specific situation and type of influence being exerted. We suggested that deviants are influenced less than nondeviants in most situations, but that deviants also avoid appearing different in public. When there is little or no direct interaction or when responses are private, deviants succumb less to social influence. The more contact there is, the more threatening the situation, the more dominant the avoidance tendency becomes, and the more they give in to the influence attempt.

This analysis was proposed after most of the results of the

research were considered. Thus, it naturally fits the results, but it has not been sufficiently tested. Additional research should concentrate on providing such a test. If the explanation is supported by the data, it would then be important to investigate why deviants in general are less persuasible, and what situations maximize their persuasibility.

Some Questions

These studies have attempted to investigate deviancy in an experimental paradigm. To do this we have produced feelings of deviancy by a complex experimental manipulation. We feel that the procedure was probably quite successful in producing some kind of feelings in the subjects, and we have presented some evidence in Chapter 5 that these feelings at least resemble what we normally think of as feelings of being deviant. Nevertheless, this is obviously a very specialized and limited type of deviancy. It may well be representative of all other kinds of deviant feelings, but on the other hand it may not be. Before the findings reported here can be generalized very far, it would be desirable to manipulate deviancy in some other manner, ideally as different as possible from that employed here. It would also be illuminating to put natural deviants of a wide variety of types through the situations described here. Although we would expect large differences among various types, it would be very reassuring if overall the deviant groups differed from nondeviant groups in the same way as the experimentally produced deviants did in our studies.

This research has deliberately studied deviancy more or less in a vacuum. This was done to eliminate various confounding effects produced by particular types of deviancy, but in doing this we were necessarily prevented from discovering the relationship between these general feelings of deviancy and the more specific feelings produced by the particular deviant characteristic. Therefore, we have virtually no information on how important these general feelings are, when they do and do not operate, what effect they might have on people who also have specific deviant characteristics, and so on. It has been our belief that all deviants share these feelings and that the effects they produce are superimposed on effects caused by the specific attributes. This, however, remains to be tested.

Another question which we have ignored is the effect on the deviant of the presence of a group in which he is not deviant. In all of our studies, the deviant subject faces the nondeviants either alone or at best with one other person similar to him. In the real world, however, most deviants are far from unique. There is almost always a group of people who are similar to them and in which, presumably, they can at least temporarily become nondeviants. As we mentioned in Chapter 3, there seems to be a strong tendency for deviants to seek out others who are similar to them, and thus probably insulate themselves from the nondeviant, threatening society. The size, strength, and availability of such groups differ considerably for different types of deviants. There are large and reasonably strong groups of Negroes, Jews, Catholics, and of the highly intelligent. There are, in contrast, very small numbers and at best only minimal organizations of midgets, physically deformed, and foot fetishists. The existence of an accepting, organized group must be exceedingly important to a deviant and must to some extent affect his relationships to nondeviants. Just what these effects are is for the moment unknown and it would seem to be an interesting and fruitful area for further research.

We have dealt with just a small sample of the possible situations in which deviancy might produce important effects. In addition, although we have obtained a number of powerful effects, we have not investigated any of them in detail. At the beginning of this project, our chief goal was to demonstrate that deviancy is indeed an important variable and to specify some of the ways in which it operates. We hoped that this would suggest to others, and to ourselves, areas for further, more detailed, and perhaps more theoretically oriented research. As usual, many questions have been raised and few answered. Since this was, in part, our goal we are satisfied with it as long as we have managed to interest others enough so that they will help us try to find the answers.

REFERENCES

Allport, G. W. *ABC's of scapegoating.* Chicago: Central YMCA College, 1944.

Asch, S. E. Effects of group pressure upon the modification and distortion of judgments. In Harold Guetzkow (Ed.), *Groups, leadership and men.* Pittsburgh: Carnegie Press, 1951.

Bandura, A. & Walters, R. H. *Social learning and personality development.* New York: Holt, Rinehart & Winston, 1963.

Becker, H. S. *Outsiders: Studies in the sociology of deviance.* New York: The Free Press, 1963.

Becker, S. W. & Carroll, Jean Ordinal position and conformity. *Journal of Abnormal and Social Psychology,* 1962, **65,** 129-131.

Berkowitz, L. *Aggression: A social psychological analysis.* New York: McGraw-Hill, 1962.

Bramel, D. A dissonance theory approach to defensive projection. *Journal of Abnormal and Social Psychology,* 1962, **64,** 121-129.

Buss, A. H. *The psychology of aggression.* New York: Wiley, 1961.

Canon, L. K. Self-confidence and selective exposure to information. In L. Festinger (Ed.), *Conflict, decision and dissonance.* Stanford, California: Stanford University Press, 1964.

Carlsmith, J. M. & Gross, A. E., Some effects of guilt on compliance. Unpublished manuscript, 1968.

Clinard, M. B. *Sociology of deviant behavior.* New York: Holt, Rinehart & Winston, 1963.

Crowne, D. P. & Marlowe, D. A new scale of social desirability independent of psychopathology. *Journal of Consulting Psychology,* 1960, **24,** 349-354.

Darley, J. M. & Aronson, E. Self-evaluation vs. direct anxiety, reduction as determinants of the fear-affiliation relationship. In B. Latané (Ed.), *Studies in social comparison.* New York: Academic Press, 1966, pp. 66-79.

Davis, K. Prostitution. In R. K. Merton, and R. A. Niabet (Eds.), *Contemporary social problems.* New York: Harcourt-Brace, 1961.

Deutsch, M. & Gerard, H. B. A study of normative and informational social influences upon individual judgment. *Journal of Abnormal and Social Psychology,* 1955, **51,** 629-636.

Dittes, J. E., & Kelley, H. H. Effects of different conditions of acceptance upon conformity to group norm. *Journal of Abnormal and Social Psychology*, 1956, **53,** 100-107.

Festinger, L. A theory of social comparison processes. *Human Relations*, 1954, **7,** 117-140.

Festinger, L., Gerard, H. B., Hymovitch, B., Kelley, H. H., & Raven, B. The influence process in the presence of extreme deviates. *Human Relations*, 1952, **5,** 327-346.

Festinger, L., Schachter, S. & Back, K. *Social pressures in informal groups: A study of human factors in housing.* New York: Harper, 1950.

Frazier, F. E. *The Negro in the United States.* New York: Macmillan, 1957.

Freedman, J. L. Confidence, utility, and selective exposure to information: a partial replication. *Journal of Personality and Social Psychology*, 1965, **2,** 778-780.

Freedman, J. L. & Schiffenbauer, A. I. The effect of self-image on compliance. Unpublished manuscript. 1967.

Freedman, J. L., Wallington, Sue, & Bless, Evelyn. Compliance without pressure: The effect of guilt, *Journal of Personality and Social Psychology*, 1967, **7,** 125-134.

Goffman, E. *Stigma.* New Jersey: Prentice-Hall, 1963.

Hakmiller, K. L. Need for self-evaluation, perceived similarity, and comparison choice. In B. Latané (Ed.), *Studies in social comparison.* New York: Academic Press, 1966, pp. 49-54.

Kaplan, B. *The eternal stranger: A study of Jewish life in the small community.* New York: Bookman Associates, 1957.

Kleck, R., Ono, H., & Hastorf, A. H. The effects of physical deviancy upon face-to-face interaction. *Human Relations*, 1966, **19,** 425-436.

Linde, T. F. Influence of orthopedic disability on conformity behavior. *Journal of Abnormal and Social Psychology*, 1964, **68,** 115-118.

Rechy, J. *City of Night.* New York: Grove Press, 1963.

Schachter, S. Deviation, rejection, and communication. *Journal of Abnormal and Social Psychology*, 1951, **46,** 190-208.

Schachter, S. *The psychology of affiliation.* Stanford: Stanford University Press, 1959.

Schachter, S., Ellertson, N., McBride, Dorothy, & Gregory, Doris. An experimental study of cohesiveness and productivity. *Human Relations*, 1951, **4,** 229-238.

Smith, B. *Police systems in the United States.* (Rev. ed.) New York: 1960.

Stonequist, E. V. *The marginal man.* New York: Charles Scribner, 1937.

Terman, L. M. *et al. Genetic studies of genius.* Stanford: Stanford University Press, 1925.

Zimbardo, P., & Formica, R. Emotional comparison and self-esteem as determinants of affiliation. *Journal of Personality*, 1963, **31,** 141-162.

INDEX